The
Poetry of
Longfellow

The
Poetry of
Longfellow

This edition published in 2020 by Arcturus Publishing Limited
26/27 Bickels Yard, 151–153 Bermondsey Street,
London SE1 3HA

Copyright © Arcturus Holdings Limited

AD007500US

Printed in the UK

Contents

Introduction

In his lifetime, Henry Wadsworth Longfellow (1807–82) was a celebrity, both in his native America and in Europe. His poetry was widely admired: by Nathaniel Hawthorne, Abraham Lincoln, Charles Dickens, and Queen Victoria, who invited him to Windsor Castle in 1868, as well as by literary critics and the people who bought his published works in their thousands. His writing made him rich. It is said that Alfred, Lord Tennyson, another admirer of his work and England's poet laureate at the time, once boasted that he earned two thousand pounds a year from his poetry, before adding, "But Longfellow, alas, receives three thousand"— that's roughly $500,000 today!

Born into a prominent family in Portland, Maine (then part of Massachusetts), Longfellow's upbringing, remembered in the poem "My Lost Youth," was loving and privileged. Enjoying the finest New England education, he found his vocation early, publishing his first poem "The Battle of Lovell's Pond" aged 14. Professorships at Bowdoin College, which he attended, and then Harvard, enabled him to continue his writing and to travel across Europe. For the young scholar, it was a magical time, drinking in the meter and rhythm of European literature and language, exchanging stories of his childhood in Portland with writers and artists from Rome, London, Paris, and Amsterdam.

Longfellow returned home from a trip to Europe in the autumn of 1836, following the death of his first wife, Mary. At this point, critics claim that a combination of his grief, his deep knowledge of European literature, and the responsibility that came with his appointment to the Chair of Modern Languages at Harvard fueled an outpouring of creativity that propelled him to success. His first collection, *Voices in the Night*, which included "A Psalm of Life," appeared in 1839 and was an immediate success.

This was followed three years later by *Ballads and Other Poems*, from which "The Wreck of the Hesperus" and "The Village Blacksmith" were memorized and recited by families across the country for their evening's entertainment. Longfellow's poems, with their musical rhythms and regular rhymes, used European poetic traditions to address uniquely American subjects. Better still, they were easy to remember and fun to recite, earning him membership of a group of writers known as the "fireside poets."

In 1843, he married his second wife, Fanny Appleton. They set up home near the Harvard campus in Cambridge, Massachusetts, and he began the most prolific part of his literary life. While bringing up their family of six children, Longfellow wrote some of the most celebrated American lyrical poems: including "Evangeline: A Tale of Acadie" in 1847, "The Song of Hiawatha" in 1855 and "Paul Revere's Ride" in 1860, works that marked Longfellow out as the favorite poet of his day.

Then, in 1861, tragedy struck when his wife died in a house fire. Following this, the poet's output declined, though his popularity did not. After a period of mourning, he returned to the literary circuit, where his charm, good manners, and distinguished white beard, grown to cover the burn scars suffered when he tried to save his wife from the fire, made him a popular guest. His 75th birthday, in February 1882, was marked by a day of national celebration, but less than a month later he died of phlebitis.

The Battle of Lovell's Pond

Cold, cold is the north wind and rude is the blast
That sweeps like a hurricane loudly and fast,
As it moans through the tall waving pines lone and drear,
Sighs a requiem sad o'er the warrior's bier.

The war-whoop is still, and the savage's yell
Has sunk into silence along the wild dell;
The din of the battle, the tumult, is o'er,
And the war-clarion's voice is now heard no more.

The warriors that fought for their country, and bled,
Have sunk to their rest; the damp earth is their bed;
No stone tells the place where their ashes repose,
Nor points out the spot from the graves of their foes.

They died in their glory, surrounded by fame,
And Victory's loud trump their death did proclaim;
They are dead; but they live in each Patriot's breast,
And their names are engraven on honor's bright crest.

Autumn

With what a glory comes and goes the year!
The buds of spring, those beautiful harbingers
Of sunny skies and cloudless times, enjoy
Life's newness, and earth's garniture spread out;
And when the silver habit of the clouds
Comes down upon the autumn sun, and with
A sober gladness the old year takes up
His bright inheritance of golden fruits,
A pomp and pageant fill the splendid scene.

There is a beautiful spirit breathing now
Its mellow richness on the clustered trees,
And, from a beaker full of richest dyes,
Pouring new glory on the autumn woods,
And dipping in warm light the pillared clouds.
Morn on the mountain, like a summer bird,
Lifts up her purple wing, and in the vales
The gentle wind, a sweet and passionate wooer,
Kisses the blushing leaf, and stirs up life
Within the solemn woods of ash deep-crimsoned,
And silver beech, and maple yellow-leaved,
Where Autumn, like a faint old man, sits down
By the wayside a-weary. Through the trees
The golden robin moves. The purple finch,
That on wild cherry and red cedar feeds,
A winter bird, comes with its plaintive whistle,
And pecks by the witch-hazel, whilst aloud
From cottage roofs the warbling bluebird sings,
And merrily, with oft-repeated stroke,
Sounds from the threshing-floor the busy flail.

Oh, what a glory doth this world put on
For him who, with a fervent heart, goes forth
Under the bright and glorious sky, and looks
On duties well performed, and days well spent!
For him the wind, ay, and the yellow leaves,
Shall have a voice, and give him eloquent teachings.
He shall so hear the solemn hymn that Death
Has lifted up for all, that he shall go
To his long resting-place without a tear.

Woods in Winter

When winter winds are piercing chill,
    And through the hawthorn blows the gale,
With solemn feet I tread the hill,
    That overbrows the lonely vale.

O'er the bare upland, and away
    Through the long reach of desert woods,
The embracing sunbeams chastely play,
    And gladden these deep solitudes.

Where, twisted round the barren oak,
    The summer vine in beauty clung,
And summer winds the stillness broke,
    The crystal icicle is hung.

Where, from their frozen urns, mute springs
    Pour out the river's gradual tide,
Shrilly the skater's iron rings,
    And voices fill the woodland side.

Alas! how changed from the fair scene,
    When birds sang out their mellow lay,
And winds were soft, and woods were green,
    And the song ceased not with the day!

But still wild music is abroad,
    Pale, desert woods! within your crowd;
And gathering winds, in hoarse accord,
    Amid the vocal reeds pipe loud.

Chill airs and wintry winds! my ear
    Has grown familiar with your song;
I hear it in the opening year,
    I listen, and it cheers me long.

Sunrise on the Hills

I stood upon the hills, when heaven's wide arch
Was glorious with the sun's returning march,
And woods were brightened, and soft gales
Went forth to kiss the sun-clad vales.
The clouds were far beneath me; bathed in light,
They gathered mid-way round the wooded height,
And, in their fading glory, shone
Like hosts in battle overthrown.
As many a pinnacle, with shifting glance,
Through the gray mist thrust up its shattered lance,
And rocking on the cliff was left
The dark pine blasted, bare, and cleft.
The veil of cloud was lifted, and below
Glowed the rich valley, and the river's flow
Was darkened by the forest's shade,
Or glistened in the white cascade;
Where upward, in the mellow blush of day,
The noisy bittern wheeled his spiral way.

I heard the distant waters dash,
I saw the current whirl and flash,
And richly, by the blue lake's silver beach,
The woods were bending with a silent reach.
Then o'er the vale, with gentle swell,
The music of the village bell
Came sweetly to the echo-giving hills;
And the wild horn, whose voice the woodland fills,
Was ringing to the merry shout,
That faint and far the glen sent out,

Where, answering to the sudden shot, thin smoke,
Through thick-leaved branches, from the dingle broke.

     If thou art worn and hard beset
With sorrows, that thou wouldst forget,
If thou wouldst read a lesson, that will keep
Thy heart from fainting and thy soul from sleep,
Go to the woods and hills! No tears
Dim the sweet look that Nature wears.

Footsteps of Angels

When the hours of Day are numbered,
 And the voices of the Night
Wake the better soul, that slumbered,
 To a holy, calm delight;

Ere the evening lamps are lighted,
 And, like phantoms grim and tall,
Shadows from the fitful firelight
 Dance upon the parlor wall;

Then the forms of the departed
 Enter at the open door;
The beloved, the true-hearted,
 Come to visit me once more;

He, the young and strong, who cherished
 Noble longings for the strife,
By the roadside fell and perished,
 Weary with the march of life!

They, the holy ones and weakly,
 Who the cross of suffering bore,
Folded their pale hands so meekly,
 Spake with us on earth no more!

And with them the Being Beauteous,
 Who unto my youth was given,
More than all things else to love me,
 And is now a saint in heaven.

With a slow and noiseless footstep
    Comes that messenger divine,
Takes the vacant chair beside me,
    Lays her gentle hand in mine.

And she sits and gazes at me
    With those deep and tender eyes,
Like the stars, so still and saint-like,
    Looking downward from the skies.

Uttered not, yet comprehended,
    Is the spirit's voiceless prayer,
Soft rebukes, in blessings ended,
    Breathing from her lips of air.

Oh, though oft depressed and lonely,
    All my fears are laid aside,
If I but remember only
    Such as these have lived and died!

A Psalm of Life

What the Heart of the Young Man Said to the Psalmist

Tell me not, in mournful numbers,
    Life is but an empty dream!
For the soul is dead that slumbers,
    And things are not what they seem.

Life is real! Life is earnest!
    And the grave is not its goal;
Dust thou art, to dust returnest,
    Was not spoken of the soul.

Not enjoyment, and not sorrow,
    Is our destined end or way;
But to act, that each to-morrow
    Find us farther than to-day.

Art is long, and Time is fleeting,
    And our hearts, though stout and brave,
Still, like muffled drums, are beating
    Funeral marches to the grave.

In the world's broad field of battle,
    In the bivouac of Life,
Be not like dumb, driven cattle!
    Be a hero in the strife!

Trust no Future, howe'er pleasant!
    Let the dead Past bury its dead!

Act,—act in the living Present!
      Heart within, and God o'erhead!

Lives of great men all remind us
      We can make our lives sublime,
And, departing, leave behind us
      Footprints on the sands of time;

Footprints, that perhaps another,
      Sailing o'er life's solemn main,
A forlorn and shipwrecked brother,
      Seeing, shall take heart again.

Let us, then, be up and doing,
      With a heart for any fate;
Still achieving, still pursuing,
      Learn to labor and to wait.

Flowers

Spake full well, in language quaint and olden,
    One who dwelleth by the castled Rhine,
When he called the flowers, so blue and golden,
    Stars, that in earth's firmament do shine.

Stars they are, wherein we read our history,
    As astrologers and seers of eld;
Yet not wrapped about with awful mystery,
    Like the burning stars, which they beheld.

Wondrous truths, and manifold as wondrous,
    God hath written in those stars above;
But not less in the bright flowerets under us
    Stands the revelation of his love.

Bright and glorious is that revelation,
    Written all over this great world of ours;
Making evident our own creation,
    In these stars of earth, these golden flowers.

And the Poet, faithful and far-seeing,
    Sees, alike in stars and flowers, a part
Of the self-same, universal being,
    Which is throbbing in his brain and heart.

Gorgeous flowerets in the sunlight shining,
    Blossoms flaunting in the eye of day,
Tremulous leaves, with soft and silver lining,
    Buds that open only to decay;

Brilliant hopes, all woven in gorgeous tissues,
　　Flaunting gayly in the golden light;
Large desires, with most uncertain issues,
　　Tender wishes, blossoming at night!

These in flowers and men are more than seeming,
　　Workings are they of the self-same powers,
Which the Poet, in no idle dreaming,
　　Seeth in himself and in the flowers.

Everywhere about us are they glowing,
　　Some like stars, to tell us Spring is born;
Others, their blue eyes with tears o'er-flowing,
　　Stand like Ruth amid the golden corn;

Not alone in Spring's armorial bearing,
　　And in Summer's green-emblazoned field,
But in arms of brave old Autumn's wearing,
　　In the centre of his brazen shield;

Not alone in meadows and green alleys,
　　On the mountain-top, and by the brink
Of sequestered pools in woodland valleys,
　　Where the slaves of nature stoop to drink;

Not alone in her vast dome of glory,
　　Not on graves of bird and beast alone,
But in old cathedrals, high and hoary,
　　On the tombs of heroes, carved in stone;

In the cottage of the rudest peasant,
　　In ancestral homes, whose crumbling towers,

Speaking of the Past unto the Present,
    Tell us of the ancient Games of Flowers;

In all places, then, and in all seasons,
    Flowers expand their light and soul-like wings,
Teaching us, by most persuasive reasons,
    How akin they are to human things.

And with childlike, credulous affection,
    We behold their tender buds expand;
Emblems of our own great resurrection,
    Emblems of the bright and better land.

The Beleaguered City

I have read, in some old, marvellous tale,
    Some legend strange and vague,
That a midnight host of spectres pale
    Beleaguered the walls of Prague.

Beside the Moldau's rushing stream,
    With the wan moon overhead,
There stood, as in an awful dream,
    The army of the dead.

White as a sea-fog, landward bound,
    The spectral camp was seen,
And, with a sorrowful, deep sound,
    The river flowed between.

No other voice nor sound was there,
    No drum, nor sentry's pace;
The mist-like banners clasped the air,
    As clouds with clouds embrace.

But when the old cathedral bell
    Proclaimed the morning prayer,
The white pavilions rose and fell
    On the alarmèd air.

Down the broad valley fast and far
    The troubled army fled;
Up rose the glorious morning star,
    The ghastly host was dead.

I have read, in the marvellous heart of man,
    That strange and mystic scroll,
That an army of phantoms vast and wan
    Beleaguer the human soul.

Encamped beside Life's rushing stream,
    In Fancy's misty light,
Gigantic shapes and shadows gleam
    Portentous through the night.

Upon its midnight battle-ground
    The spectral camp is seen,
And, with a sorrowful, deep sound,
    Flows the River of Life between.

No other voice nor sound is there,
    In the army of the grave;
No other challenge breaks the air,
    But the rushing of Life's wave.

And when the solemn and deep church-bell
    Entreats the soul to pray,
The midnight phantoms feel the spell,
    The shadows sweep away.

Down the broad Vale of Tears afar
    The spectral camp is fled;
Faith shineth as a morning star,
    Our ghastly fears are dead.

Hymn to the Night

Aspasie, trillistos.

I heard the trailing garments of the Night
     Sweep through her marble halls!
I saw her sable skirts all fringed with light
     From the celestial walls!

I felt her presence, by its spell of might,
     Stoop o'er me from above;
The calm, majestic presence of the Night,
     As of the one I love.

I heard the sounds of sorrow and delight,
     The manifold, soft chimes,
That fill the haunted chambers of the Night,
     Like some old poet's rhymes.

From the cool cisterns of the midnight air
     My spirit drank repose;
The fountain of perpetual peace flows there,—
     From those deep cisterns flows.

O holy Night! from thee I learn to bear
     What man has borne before!
Thou layest thy finger on the lips of Care,
     And they complain no more.

Peace! Peace! Orestes-like I breathe this prayer!
     Descend with broad-winged flight,

The welcome, the thrice-prayed for, the most fair,
  The best-beloved Night!

The Light of Stars

The night is come, but not too soon;
    And sinking silently,
All silently, the little moon
    Drops down behind the sky.

There is no light in earth or heaven
    But the cold light of stars;
And the first watch of night is given
    To the red planet Mars.

Is it the tender star of love?
    The star of love and dreams?
O no! from that blue tent above,
    A hero's armor gleams.

And earnest thoughts within me rise,
    When I behold afar,
Suspended in the evening skies,
    The shield of that red star.

O star of strength! I see thee stand
    And smile upon my pain;
Thou beckonest with thy mailèd hand,
    And I am strong again.

Within my breast there is no light
    But the cold light of stars;
I give the first watch of the night
    To the red planet Mars.

The star of the unconquered will,
　　He rises in my breast,
Serene, and resolute, and still,
　　And calm, and self-possessed.

And thou, too, whosoe'er thou art,
　　That readest this brief psalm,
As one by one thy hopes depart,
　　Be resolute and calm.

O fear not in a world like this,
　　And thou shalt know erelong,
Know how sublime a thing it is
　　To suffer and be strong.

The Reaper and the Flowers

There is a Reaper, whose name is Death,
    And, with his sickle keen,
He reaps the bearded grain at a breath,
    And the flowers that grow between.

"Shall I have naught that is fair?" saith he;
    "Have naught but the bearded grain?
Though the breath of these flowers is sweet to me,
    I will give them all back again."

He gazed at the flowers with tearful eyes,
    He kissed their drooping leaves;
It was for the Lord of Paradise
    He bound them in his sheaves.

"My Lord has need of these flowerets gay,"
    The Reaper said, and smiled;
"Dear tokens of the earth are they,
    Where He was once a child.

"They shall all bloom in fields of light,
    Transplanted by my care,
And saints, upon their garments white,
    These sacred blossoms wear."

And the mother gave, in tears and pain,
    The flowers she most did love;
She knew she should find them all again
    In the fields of light above.

Oh, not in cruelty, not in wrath,
    The Reaper came that day;
'Twas an angel visited the green earth,
    And took the flowers away.

The Skeleton in Armor

"Speak! speak! thou fearful guest!
Who, with thy hollow breast
Still in rude armor drest,
    Comest to daunt me!
Wrapt not in Eastern balms,
But with thy fleshless palms
Stretched, as if asking alms,
    Why dost thou haunt me?"

Then, from those cavernous eyes
Pale flashes seemed to rise,
As when the Northern skies
    Gleam in December;
And, like the water's flow
Under December's snow,
Came a dull voice of woe
    From the heart's chamber.

"I was a Viking old!
My deeds, though manifold,
No Skald in song has told,
    No Saga taught thee!
Take heed, that in thy verse
Thou dost the tale rehearse,
Else dread a dead man's curse;
    For this I sought thee.

"Far in the Northern Land,
By the wild Baltic's strand,
I, with my childish hand,

Tamed the gerfalcon;
And, with my skates fast-bound,
Skimmed the half-frozen Sound,
That the poor whimpering hound
    Trembled to walk on.

"Oft to his frozen lair
Tracked I the grisly bear,
While from my path the hare
    Fled like a shadow;
Oft through the forest dark
Followed the were-wolf's bark,
Until the soaring lark
    Sang from the meadow.

"But when I older grew,
Joining a corsair's crew,
O'er the dark sea I flew
    With the marauders.
Wild was the life we led;
Many the souls that sped,
Many the hearts that bled,
    By our stern orders.

"Many a wassail-bout
Wore the long Winter out;
Often our midnight shout
    Set the cocks crowing,
As we the Berserk's tale
Measured in cups of ale,
Draining the oaken pail,
    Filled to o'erflowing.

"Once as I told in glee
Tales of the stormy sea,
Soft eyes did gaze on me,
        Burning yet tender;
And as the white stars shine
On the dark Norway pine,
On that dark heart of mine
        Fell their soft splendor.

"I wooed the blue-eyed maid,
Yielding, yet half afraid,
And in the forest's shade
        Our vows were plighted.
Under its loosened vest
Fluttered her little breast,
Like birds within their nest
        By the hawk frighted.

"Bright in her father's hall
Shields gleamed upon the wall,
Loud sang the minstrels all,
        Chanting his glory;
When of old Hildebrand
I asked his daughter's hand,
Mute did the minstrels stand
        To hear my story.

"While the brown ale he quaffed,
Loud then the champion laughed,
And as the wind-gusts waft
        The sea-foam brightly,

So the loud laugh of scorn,
Out of those lips unshorn,
From the deep drinking-horn
    Blew the foam lightly.

"She was a Prince's child,
I but a Viking wild,
And though she blushed and smiled,
    I was discarded!
Should not the dove so white
Follow the sea-mew's flight,
Why did they leave that night
    Her nest unguarded?

"Scarce had I put to sea,
Bearing the maid with me,
Fairest of all was she
    Among the Norsemen!
When on the white sea-strand,
Waving his armed hand,
Saw we old Hildebrand,
    With twenty horsemen.

"Then launched they to the blast,
Bent like a reed each mast,
Yet we were gaining fast,
    When the wind failed us;
And with a sudden flaw
Came round the gusty Skaw,
So that our foe we saw
    Laugh as he hailed us.

"And as to catch the gale
Round veered the flapping sail,
'Death!' was the helmsman's hail,
　　'Death without quarter!'
Mid-ships with iron keel
Struck we her ribs of steel;
Down her black hulk did reel
　　Through the black water!

"As with his wings aslant,
Sails the fierce cormorant,
Seeking some rocky haunt,
　　With his prey laden,—
So toward the open main,
Beating to sea again,
Through the wild hurricane,
　　Bore I the maiden.

"Three weeks we westward bore,
And when the storm was o'er,
Cloud-like we saw the shore
　　Stretching to leeward;
There for my lady's bower
Built I the lofty tower,
Which, to this very hour,
　　Stands looking seaward.

"There lived we many years;
Time dried the maiden's tears;
She had forgot her fears,
　　She was a mother;
Death closed her mild blue eyes,

Under that tower she lies;
Ne'er shall the sun arise
    On such another!

"Still grew my bosom then,
Still as a stagnant fen!
Hateful to me were men,
    The sunlight hateful!
In the vast forest here,
Clad in my warlike gear,
Fell I upon my spear,
    Oh, death was grateful!

"Thus, seamed with many scars,
Bursting these prison bars,
Up to its native stars
    My soul ascended!
There from the flowing bowl
Deep drinks the warrior's soul,
Skoal! to the Northland! skoal!"
    Thus the tale ended.

The Wreck of the Hesperus

It was the schooner Hesperus,
    That sailed the wintry sea;
And the skipper had taken his little daughtèr,
    To bear him company.

Blue were her eyes as the fairy-flax,
    Her cheeks like the dawn of day,
And her bosom white as the hawthorn buds,
    That ope in the month of May.

The skipper he stood beside the helm,
    His pipe was in his mouth,
And he watched how the veering flaw did blow
    The smoke now West, now South.

Then up and spake an old Sailòr,
    Had sailed to the Spanish Main,
"I pray thee, put into yonder port,
    For I fear a hurricane.

"Last night, the moon had a golden ring,
    And to-night no moon we see!"
The skipper, he blew a whiff from his pipe,
    And a scornful laugh laughed he.

Colder and louder blew the wind,
    A gale from the Northeast,
The snow fell hissing in the brine,
    And the billows frothed like yeast.

Down came the storm, and smote amain
    The vessel in its strength;
She shuddered and paused, like a frighted steed,
    Then leaped her cable's length.

"Come hither! come hither! my little daughtèr,
    And do not tremble so;
For I can weather the roughest gale
    That ever wind did blow."

He wrapped her warm in his seaman's coat
    Against the stinging blast;
He cut a rope from a broken spar,
    And bound her to the mast.

"O father! I hear the church-bells ring,
    Oh say, what may it be?"
"'Tis a fog-bell on a rock-bound coast!"—
    And he steered for the open sea.

"O father! I hear the sound of guns,
    Oh say, what may it be?"
"Some ship in distress, that cannot live
    In such an angry sea!"

"O father! I see a gleaming light,
    Oh say, what may it be?"
But the father answered never a word,
    A frozen corpse was he.

Lashed to the helm, all stiff and stark,
    With his face turned to the skies,

The lantern gleamed through the gleaming snow
        On his fixed and glassy eyes.

Then the maiden clasped her hands and prayed
        That savèd she might be;
And she thought of Christ, who stilled the wave
        On the Lake of Galilee.

And fast through the midnight dark and drear,
        Through the whistling sleet and snow,
Like a sheeted ghost, the vessel swept
        Tow'rds the reef of Norman's Woe.

And ever the fitful gusts between
        A sound came from the land;
It was the sound of the trampling surf
        On the rocks and the hard sea-sand.

The breakers were right beneath her bows,
        She drifted a dreary wreck,
And a whooping billow swept the crew
        Like icicles from her deck.

She struck where the white and fleecy waves
        Looked soft as carded wool,
But the cruel rocks, they gored her side
        Like the horns of an angry bull.

Her rattling shrouds, all sheathed in ice,
        With the masts went by the board;
Like a vessel of glass, she stove and sank,
        Ho! ho! the breakers roared!

At daybreak, on the bleak sea-beach,
      A fisherman stood aghast,
To see the form of a maiden fair,
      Lashed close to a drifting mast.

The salt sea was frozen on her breast,
      The salt tears in her eyes;
And he saw her hair, like the brown sea-weed,
      On the billows fall and rise.

Such was the wreck of the Hesperus,
      In the midnight and the snow!
Christ save us all from a death like this,
      On the reef of Norman's Woe!

The Slave Singing at Midnight

Loud he sang the psalm of David!
He, a Negro and enslaved,
Sang of Israel's victory,
Sang of Zion, bright and free.

In that hour, when night is calmest,
Sang he from the Hebrew Psalmist,
In a voice so sweet and clear
That I could not choose but hear,

Songs of triumph, and ascriptions,
Such as reached the swart Egyptians,
When upon the Red Sea coast
Perished Pharaoh and his host.

And the voice of his devotion
Filled my soul with strange emotion;
For its tones by turns were glad,
Sweetly solemn, wildly sad.

Paul and Silas, in their prison,
Sang of Christ, the Lord arisen,
And an earthquake's arm of might
Broke their dungeon-gates at night.

But, alas! what holy angel
Brings the Slave this glad evangel?
And what earthquake's arm of might
Breaks his dungeon-gates at night?

The Witnesses

In Ocean's wide domains,
    Half buried in the sands,
Lie skeletons in chains,
    With shackled feet and hands.

Beyond the fall of dews,
    Deeper than plummet lies,
Float ships, with all their crews,
    No more to sink nor rise.

There the black Slave-ship swims,
    Freighted with human forms,
Whose fettered, fleshless limbs
    Are not the sport of storms.

These are the bones of Slaves;
    They gleam from the abyss;
They cry, from yawning waves,
    "We are the Witnesses!"

Within Earth's wide domains
    Are markets for men's lives;
Their necks are galled with chains,
    Their wrists are cramped with gyves.

Dead bodies, that the kite
    In deserts makes its prey;
Murders, that with affright
    Scare school-boys from their play!

All evil thoughts and deeds;
 Anger, and lust, and pride;
The foulest, rankest weeds,
 That choke Life's groaning tide!

These are the woes of Slaves;
 They glare from the abyss;
They cry, from unknown graves,
 "We are the Witnesses!"

The Village Blacksmith

Under a spreading chestnut-tree
    The village smithy stands;
The smith, a mighty man is he,
    With large and sinewy hands,
And the muscles of his brawny arms
    Are strong as iron bands.

His hair is crisp, and black, and long;
    His face is like the tan;
His brow is wet with honest sweat,
    He earns whate'er he can,
And looks the whole world in the face,
    For he owes not any man.

Week in, week out, from morn till night,
    You can hear his bellows blow;
You can hear him swing his heavy sledge,
    With measured beat and slow,
Like a sexton ringing the village bell,
    When the evening sun is low.

And children coming home from school
    Look in at the open door;
They love to see the flaming forge,
    And hear the bellows roar,
And catch the burning sparks that fly
    Like chaff from a threshing-floor.

He goes on Sunday to the church,
    And sits among his boys;

He hears the parson pray and preach,
    He hears his daughter's voice
Singing in the village choir,
    And it makes his heart rejoice.

It sounds to him like her mother's voice
    Singing in Paradise!
He needs must think of her once more,
    How in the grave she lies;
And with his hard, rough hand he wipes
    A tear out of his eyes.

Toiling,—rejoicing,—sorrowing,
    Onward through life he goes;
Each morning sees some task begin,
    Each evening sees it close;
Something attempted, something done,
    Has earned a night's repose.

Thanks, thanks to thee, my worthy friend,
    For the lesson thou hast taught!
Thus at the flaming forge of life
    Our fortunes must be wrought;
Thus on its sounding anvil shaped
    Each burning deed and thought.

Endymion

The rising moon has hid the stars;
Her level rays, like golden bars,
    Lie on the landscape green,
    With shadows brown between.

And silver white the river gleams,
As if Diana, in her dreams,
    Had dropt her silver bow
    Upon the meadows low.

On such a tranquil night as this,
She woke Endymion with a kiss,
    When, sleeping in the grove,
    He dreamed not of her love.

Like Dian's kiss, unasked, unsought,
Love gives itself, but is not bought;
    Nor voice, nor sound betrays
    Its deep, impassioned gaze.

It comes,—the beautiful, the free,
The crown of all humanity,—
    In silence and alone
    To seek the elected one.

It lifts the boughs, whose shadows deep
Are Life's oblivion, the soul's sleep,
    And kisses the closed eyes
    Of him, who slumbering lies.

O weary hearts! O slumbering eyes!
O drooping souls, whose destinies
     Are fraught with fear and pain,
     Ye shall be loved again!

No one is so accursed by fate,
No one so utterly desolate,
     But some heart, though unknown,
     Responds unto his own.

Responds,—as if with unseen wings,
An angel touched its quivering strings;
     And whispers, in its song,
     "'Where hast thou stayed so long?"

The Rainy Day

The day is cold, and dark, and dreary;
It rains, and the wind is never weary;
The vine still clings to the mouldering wall,
But at every gust the dead leaves fall,
    And the day is dark and dreary.

My life is cold, and dark, and dreary;
It rains, and the wind is never weary;
My thoughts still cling to the mouldering Past,
But the hopes of youth fall thick in the blast,
    And the days are dark and dreary.

Be still, sad heart! and cease repining;
Behind the clouds is the sun still shining;
Thy fate is the common fate of all,
Into each life some rain must fall,
    Some days must be dark and dreary.

To the River Charles

River! that in silence windest
     Through the meadows, bright and free,
Till at length thy rest thou findest
     In the bosom of the sea!

Four long years of mingled feeling,
     Half in rest, and half in strife,
I have seen thy waters stealing
     Onward, like the stream of life.

Thou hast taught me, Silent River!
     Many a lesson, deep and long;
Thou hast been a generous giver;
     I can give thee but a song.

Oft in sadness and in illness,
     I have watched thy current glide,
Till the beauty of its stillness
     Overflowed me, like a tide.

And in better hours and brighter,
     When I saw thy waters gleam,
I have felt my heart beat lighter,
     And leap onward with thy stream.

Not for this alone I love thee,
     Nor because thy waves of blue
From celestial seas above thee
     Take their own celestial hue.

Where yon shadowy woodlands hide thee,
    And thy waters disappear,
Friends I love have dwelt beside thee,
    And have made thy margin dear.

More than this;—thy name reminds me
    Of three friends, all true and tried;
And that name, like magic, binds me
    Closer, closer to thy side.

Friends my soul with joy remembers!
    How like quivering flames they start,
When I fan the living embers
    On the hearth-stone of my heart!

'Tis for this, thou Silent River!
    That my spirit leans to thee;
Thou hast been a generous giver,
    Take this idle song from me.

Mezzo Cammin

Half of my life is gone, and I have let
      The years slip from me and have not fulfilled
      The aspiration of my youth, to build
      Some tower of song with lofty parapet.
Not indolence, nor pleasure, nor the fret
      Of restless passions that would not be stilled,
      But sorrow, and a care that almost killed,
      Kept me from what I may accomplish yet;
Though, half-way up the hill, I see the Past
      Lying beneath me with its sounds and sights,—
      A city in the twilight dim and vast,
With smoking roofs, soft bells, and gleaming lights,—
      And hear above me on the autumnal blast
      The cataract of Death far thundering from the
         heights.

Excelsior

The shades of night were falling fast,
As through an Alpine village passed
A youth, who bore, 'mid snow and ice,
A banner with the strange device,
    Excelsior!

His brow was sad; his eye beneath,
Flashed like a falchion from its sheath,
And like a silver clarion rung
The accents of that unknown tongue,
    Excelsior!

In happy homes he saw the light
Of household fires gleam warm and bright;
Above, the spectral glaciers shone,
And from his lips escaped a groan,
    Excelsior!

"Try not the Pass!" the old man said;
"Dark lowers the tempest overhead,
The roaring torrent is deep and wide!
And loud that clarion voice replied,
    Excelsior!

"Oh stay," the maiden said, "and rest
Thy weary head upon this breast!"
A tear stood in his bright blue eye,
But still he answered, with a sigh,
    Excelsior!

"Beware the pine-tree's withered branch!
Beware the awful avalanche!"
This was the peasant's last Good-night,
A voice replied, far up the height,
    Excelsior!

At break of day, as heavenward
The pious monks of Saint Bernard
Uttered the oft-repeated prayer,
A voice cried through the startled air,
    Excelsior!

A traveller, by the faithful hound,
Half-buried in the snow was found,
Still grasping in his hand of ice
That banner with the strange device,
    Excelsior!

There in the twilight cold and gray,
Lifeless, but beautiful, he lay,
And from the sky, serene and far,
A voice fell, like a falling star,
    Excelsior!

The Belfry of Bruges

In the market-place of Bruges stands the belfry old and
brown;
Thrice consumed and thrice rebuilded, still it watches o'er
the town.

As the summer morn was breaking, on that lofty tower I
stood,
And the world threw off the darkness, like the weeds of
widowhood.

Thick with towns and hamlets studded, and with streams
and vapors gray,
Like a shield embossed with silver, round and vast the
landscape lay.

At my feet the city slumbered. From its chimneys, here
and there,
Wreaths of snow-white smoke, ascending, vanished,
ghost-like, into air.

Not a sound rose from the city at that early morning
hour,
But I heard a heart of iron beating in the ancient
tower.

From their nests beneath the rafters sang the swallows
wild and high;
And the world, beneath me sleeping, seemed more distant
than the sky.

Then most musical and solemn, bringing back the olden
times,

With their strange, unearthly changes rang the melan-
  choly chimes,

Like the psalms from some old cloister, when the nuns
  sing in the choir;
And the great bell tolled among them, like the chanting
  of a friar.

Visions of the days departed, shadowy phantoms filled my
  brain;
They who live in history only seemed to walk the earth
  again;

All the Foresters of Flanders,—mighty Baldwin Bras de
  Fer,
Lyderick du Bucq and Cressy Philip, Guy de Dampierre.

I beheld the pageants splendid that adorned those days of
  old;
Stately dames, like queens attended, knights who bore the
  Fleece of Gold

Lombard and Venetian merchants with deep-laden argo-
  sies;
Ministers from twenty nations; more than royal pomp and
  ease.

I beheld proud Maximilian, kneeling humbly on the
  ground;
I beheld the gentle Mary, hunting with her hawk and
  hound;

And her lighted bridal-chamber, where a duke slept with
  the queen,

And the armed guard around them, and the sword
   unsheathed between.

I beheld the Flemish weavers, with Namur and Juliers
   bold,
Marching homeward from the bloody battle of the Spurs
   of Gold;

Saw the light at Minnewater, saw the White Hoods
   moving west,
Saw great Artevelde victorious scale the Golden Dragon's
   nest.

And again the whiskered Spaniard all the land with terror
   smote;
And again the wild alarum sounded from the tocsin's
   throat;

Till the bell of Ghent responded o'er lagoon and dike of
   sand,
"I am Roland! I am Roland! there is victory in the land!"

Then the sound of drums aroused me. The awakened
   city's roar
Chased the phantoms I had summoned back into their
   graves once more.

Hours had passed away like minutes; and, before I was
   aware,
Lo! the shadow of the belfry crossed the sun-illumined
   square.

To the Driving Cloud

Gloomy and dark art thou, O chief of the mighty
Omahas;
Gloomy and dark as the driving cloud, whose name thou
hast taken!
Wrapped in thy scarlet blanket, I see thee stalk through
the city's
Narrow and populous streets, as once by the margin of
rivers
Stalked those birds unknown, that have left us only their
footprints.
What, in a few short years, will remain of thy race but
the footprints?

How canst thou walk these streets, who hast trod the
green turf of the prairies?
How canst thou breathe this air, who hast breathed the
sweet air of the mountains?
Ah! 'tis in vain that with lordly looks of disdain thou dost
challenge
Looks of disdain in return, and question these walls and
these pavements,
Claiming the soil for thy hunting-grounds, while down-
trodden millions
Starve in the garrets of Europe, and cry from its caverns
that they, too,
Have been created heirs of the earth, and claim its
division!

Back, then, back to thy woods in the regions west of the
Wabash!
There as a monarch thou reignest. In autumn the leaves of
the maple
Pave the floors of thy palace-halls with gold, and in
summer
Pine-trees waft through its chambers the odorous breath
of their branches.
There thou art strong and great, a hero, a tamer of horses!
There thou chasest the stately stag on the banks of the
Elkhorn,
Or by the roar of the Running-Water, or where the
Omaha
Calls thee, and leaps through the wild ravine like a brave
of the Blackfeet!

Hark! what murmurs arise from the heart of those moun-
tainous deserts?
Is it the cry of the Foxes and Crows, or the mighty
Behemoth,
Who, unharmed, on his tusks once caught the bolts of
the thunder,
And now lurks in his lair to destroy the race of the red
man?
Far more fatal to thee and thy race than the Crows and
the Foxes,
Far more fatal to thee and thy race than the tread of
Behemoth,
Lo! the big thunder-canoe, that steadily breasts the
Missouri's
Merciless current! and yonder, afar on the prairies, the
camp-fires

Gleam through the night; and the cloud of dust in the
gray of the daybreak
Marks not the buffalo's track, nor the Mandan's dexterous
horse-race;
It is a caravan, whitening the desert where dwell the
Camanches!
Ha! how the breath of these Saxons and Celts, like the
blast of the east-wind,
Drifts evermore to the west the scanty smokes of thy
wigwams!

The Arrow and the Song

I shot an arrow into the air,
It fell to earth, I knew not where;
For, so swiftly it flew, the sight
Could not follow it in its flight.

I breathed a song into the air,
It fell to earth, I knew not where;
For who has sight so keen and strong,
That it can follow the flight of song?

Long, long afterward, in an oak
I found the arrow, still unbroke;
And the song, from beginning to end,
I found again in the heart of a friend.

The Day is Done

The day is done, and the darkness
    Falls from the wings of Night,
As a feather is wafted downward
    From an eagle in his flight.

I see the lights of the village
    Gleam through the rain and the mist,
And a feeling of sadness comes o'er me
    That my soul cannot resist:

A feeling of sadness and longing,
    That is not akin to pain,
And resembles sorrow only
    As the mist resembles the rain.

Come, read to me some poem,
    Some simple and heartfelt lay,
That shall soothe this restless feeling,
    And banish the thoughts of day.

Not from the grand old masters,
    Not from the bards sublime,
Whose distant footsteps echo
    Through the corridors of Time.

For, like strains of martial music,
    Their mighty thoughts suggest
Life's endless toil and endeavor;
    And to-night I long for rest.

Read from some humbler poet,
　　Whose songs gushed from his heart,
As showers from the clouds of summer,
　　Or tears from the eyelids start;

Who, through long days of labor,
　　And nights devoid of ease,
Still heard in his soul the music
　　Of wonderful melodies.

Such songs have power to quiet
　　The restless pulse of care,
And come like the benediction
　　That follows after prayer.

Then read from the treasured volume
　　The poem of thy choice,
And lend to the rhyme of the poet
　　The beauty of thy voice.

And the night shall be filled with music
　　And the cares, that infest the day,
Shall fold their tents, like the Arabs,
　　And as silently steal away.

The Bridge

I stood on the bridge at midnight,
 As the clocks were striking the hour,
And the moon rose o'er the city,
 Behind the dark church-tower.

I saw her bright reflection
 In the waters under me,
Like a golden goblet falling
 And sinking into the sea.

And far in the hazy distance
 Of that lovely night in June,
The blaze of the flaming furnace
 Gleamed redder than the moon.

Among the long, black rafters
 The wavering shadows lay,
And the current that came from the ocean
 Seemed to lift and bear them away;

As, sweeping and eddying through them,
 Rose the belated tide,
And, streaming into the moonlight,
 The seaweed floated wide.

And like those waters rushing
 Among the wooden piers,
A flood of thoughts came o'er me
 That filled my eyes with tears.

How often, oh, how often,
    In the days that had gone by,
I had stood on that bridge at midnight
    And gazed on that wave and sky!

How often, oh, how often,
    I had wished that the ebbing tide
Would bear me away on its bosom
    O'er the ocean wild and wide!

For my heart was hot and restless,
    And my life was full of care,
And the burden laid upon me
    Seemed greater than I could bear.

But now it has fallen from me,
    It is buried in the sea;
And only the sorrow of others
    Throws its shadow over me.

Yet whenever I cross the river
    On its bridge with wooden piers,
Like the odor of brine from the ocean
    Comes the thought of other years.

And I think how many thousands
    Of care-encumbered men,
Each bearing his burden of sorrow,
    Have crossed the bridge since then.

I see the long procession
    Still passing to and fro,

The young heart hot and restless,
    And the old subdued and slow!

And forever and forever,
    As long as the river flows,
As long as the heart has passions,
    As long as life has woes;

The moon and its broken reflection
    And its shadows shall appear,
As the symbol of love in heaven,
    And its wavering image here.

The Arsenal at Springfield

This is the Arsenal. From floor to ceiling,
      Like a huge organ, rise the burnished arms;
But from their silent pipes no anthem pealing
      Startles the villages with strange alarms.

Ah! what a sound will rise, how wild and dreary,
      When the death-angel touches those swift keys!
What loud lament and dismal *Miserere*
      Will mingle with their awful symphonies!

I hear even now the infinite fierce chorus,
      The cries of agony, the endless groan,
Which, through the ages that have gone before us,
      In long reverberations reach our own.

On helm and harness rings the Saxon hammer,
      Through Cimbric forest roars the Norseman's song,
And loud, amid the universal clamor,
      O'er distant deserts sounds the Tartar gong.

I hear the Florentine, who from his palace
      Wheels out his battle-bell with dreadful din,
And Aztec priests upon their teocallis
      Beat the wild war-drums made of serpent's skin;

The tumult of each sacked and burning village;
      The shout that every prayer for mercy drowns;
The soldiers' revels in the midst of pillage;
      The wail of famine in beleaguered towns;

The bursting shell, the gateway wrenched asunder,
 The rattling musketry, the clashing blade;
And ever and anon, in tones of thunder
 The diapason of the cannonade.

Is it, O man, with such discordant noises,
 With such accursed instruments as these,
Thou drownest Nature's sweet and kindly voices,
 And jarrest the celestial harmonies?

Were half the power, that fills the world with terror,
 Were half the wealth bestowed on camps and courts,
Given to redeem the human mind from error,
 There were no need of arsenals or forts:

The warrior's name would be a name abhorred!
 And every nation, that should lift again
Its hand against a brother, on its forehead
 Would wear forevermore the curse of Cain!

Down the dark future, through long generations,
 The echoing sounds grow fainter and then cease;
And like a bell, with solemn, sweet vibrations,
 I hear once more the voice of Christ say, "Peace!"

Peace! and no longer from its brazen portals
 The blast of War's great organ shakes the skies!
But beautiful as songs of the immortals,
 The holy melodies of love arise.

Afternoon in February

The day is ending,
The night is descending;
The marsh is frozen,
The river dead.

Through clouds like ashes
The red sun flashes
On village windows
That glimmer red.

The snow recommences;
The buried fences
Mark no longer
The road o'er the plain;

While through the meadows,
Like fearful shadows,
Slowly passes
A funeral train.

The bell is pealing,
And every feeling
Within me responds
To the dismal knell;

Shadows are trailing,
My heart is bewailing
And tolling within
Like a funeral bell.

Drinking Song

Inscription for an Antique Pitcher

Come, old friend! sit down and listen!
    From the pitcher, placed between us,
How the waters laugh and glisten
    In the head of old Silenus!

Old Silenus, bloated, drunken,
    Led by his inebriate Satyrs;
On his breast his head is sunken,
    Vacantly he leers and chatters.

Fauns with youthful Bacchus follow;
    Ivy crowns that brow supernal
As the forehead of Apollo,
    And possessing youth eternal.

Round about him, fair Bacchantes,
    Bearing cymbals, flutes, and thyrses,
Wild from Naxian groves, or Zante's
    Vineyards, sing delirious verses.

Thus he won, through all the nations,
    Bloodless victories, and the farmer
Bore, as trophies and oblations,
    Vines for banners, ploughs for armor.

Judged by no o'erzealous rigor,
    Much this mystic throng expresses:

Bacchus was the type of vigor,
    And Silenus of excesses.

These are ancient ethnic revels,
    Of a faith long since forsaken;
Now the Satyrs, changed to devils,
    Frighten mortals wine-o'ertaken.

Now to rivulets from the mountains
    Point the rods of fortune-tellers;
Youth perpetual dwells in fountains,—
    Not in flasks, and casks, and cellars.

Claudius, though he sang of flagons
    And huge tankards filled with Rhenish,
From that fiery blood of dragons
    Never would his own replenish.

Even Redi, though he chaunted
    Bacchus in the Tuscan valleys,
Never drank the wine he vaunted
    In his dithyrambic sallies.

Then with water fill the pitcher
    Wreathed about with classic fables;
Ne'er Falernian threw a richer
    Light upon Lucullus' tables.

Come, old friend, sit down and listen
    As it passes thus between us,
How its wavelets laugh and glisten
    In the head of old Silenus!

The Evening Star

Lo! in the painted oriel of the West,
     Whose panes the sunken sun incarnadines,
     Like a fair lady at her casement, shines
     The evening star, the star of love and rest!
And then anon she doth herself divest
     Of all her radiant garments, and reclines
     Behind the sombre screen of yonder pines,
     With slumber and soft dreams of love oppressed.
O my beloved, my sweet Hesperus!
     My morning and my evening star of love!
     My best and gentlest lady! even thus,
As that fair planet in the sky above,
     Dost thou retire unto thy rest at night,
     And from thy darkened window fades the light.

A Gleam of Sunshine

This is the place. Stand still, my steed,
    Let me review the scene,
And summon from the shadowy Past
    The forms that once have been.

The Past and Present here unite
    Beneath Time's flowing tide,
Like footprints hidden by a brook,
    But seen on either side.

Here runs the highway to the town;
    There the green lane descends,
Through which I walked to church with thee,
    O gentlest of my friends!

The shadow of the linden-trees
    Lay moving on the grass;
Between them and the moving boughs,
    A shadow, thou didst pass.

Thy dress was like the lilies,
    And thy heart as pure as they;
One of God's holy messengers
    Did walk with me that day.

I saw the branches of the trees
    Bend down thy touch to meet,
The clover-blossoms in the grass
    Rise up to kiss thy feet.

"Sleep, sleep to-day, tormenting cares,
　　Of earth and folly born!"
Solemnly sang the village choir
　　On that sweet Sabbath morn.

Through the closed blinds the golden sun
　　Poured in a dusty beam,
Like the celestial ladder seen
　　By Jacob in his dream.

And ever and anon, the wind
　　Sweet-scented with the hay,
Turned o'er the hymn-book's fluttering leaves
　　That on the window lay.

Long was the good man's sermon,
　　Yet it seemed not so to me;
For he spake of Ruth the beautiful,
　　And still I thought of thee.

Long was the prayer he uttered,
　　Yet it seemed not so to me;
For in my heart I prayed with him,
　　And still I thought of thee.

But now, alas! the place seems changed;
　　Thou art no longer here:
Part of the sunshine of the scene
　　With thee did disappear.

Though thoughts, deep-rooted in my heart,
　　Like pine-trees dark and high,

Subdue the light of noon, and breathe
    A low and ceaseless sigh;

This memory brightens o'er the past,
    As when the sun, concealed
Behind some cloud that near us hangs,
    Shines on a distant field.

Excerpt from *Evangeline: A Tale of Acadie*

This is the forest primeval. The murmuring pines and the
    hemlocks,
Bearded with moss, and in garments green, indistinct in
    the twilight,
Stand like Druids of eld, with voices sad and prophetic,
Stand like harpers hoar, with beards that rest on their
    bosoms.
Loud from its rocky caverns, the deep-voiced neighboring
    ocean
Speaks, and in accents disconsolate answers the wail of
    the forest.

    This is the forest primeval; but where are the hearts
        that beneath it
Leaped like the roe, when he hears in the woodland the
    voice of the huntsman?
Where is the thatch-roofed village, the home of Acadian
    farmers,—
Men whose lives glided on like rivers that water the
    woodlands,
Darkened by shadows of earth, but reflecting an image of
    heaven?
Waste are those pleasant farms, and the farmers forever
    departed!
Scattered like dust and leaves, when the mighty blasts of
    October
Seize them, and whirl them aloft, and sprinkle them far
    o'er the ocean.
Naught but tradition remains of the beautiful village of
    Grand-Pré.

Ye who believe in affection that hopes, and endures,
and is patient,
Ye who believe in the beauty and strength of woman's
devotion,
List to the mournful tradition, still sung by the pines of
the forest;
List to a Tale of Love in Acadie, home of the happy.

The Builders

All are architects of Fate,
    Working in these walls of Time;
Some with massive deeds and great,
    Some with ornaments of rhyme.

Nothing useless is, or low;
    Each thing in its place is best;
And what seems but idle show
    Strengthens and supports the rest.

For the structure that we raise,
    Time is with materials filled;
Our to-days and yesterdays
    Are the blocks with which we build.

Truly shape and fashion these;
    Leave no yawning gaps between;
Think not, because no man sees,
    Such things will remain unseen.

In the elder days of Art,
    Builders wrought with greatest care
Each minute and unseen part;
    For the Gods see everywhere.

Let us do our work as well,
    Both the unseen and the seen;
Make the house, where Gods may dwell,
    Beautiful, entire, and clean.

Else our lives are incomplete,
        Standing in these walls of Time,
Broken stairways, where the feet
        Stumble as they seek to climb.

Build to-day, then, strong and sure,
        With a firm and ample base;
And ascending and secure
        Shall to-morrow find its place.

Thus alone can we attain
        To those turrets, where the eye
Sees the world as one vast plain,
        And one boundless reach of sky.

The Fire of Drift-Wood

Devereux Farm, Near Marblehead.

We sat within the farm-house old,
　　Whose windows, looking o'er the bay,
Gave to the sea-breeze damp and cold,
　　An easy entrance, night and day.

Not far away we saw the port,
　　The strange, old-fashioned, silent town,
The lighthouse, the dismantled fort,
　　The wooden houses, quaint and brown.

We sat and talked until the night,
　　Descending, filled the little room;
Our faces faded from the sight,
　　Our voices only broke the gloom.

We spake of many a vanished scene,
　　Of what we once had thought and said,
Of what had been, and might have been,
　　And who was changed, and who was dead;

And all that fills the hearts of friends,
　　When first they feel, with secret pain,
Their lives thenceforth have separate ends,
　　And never can be one again;

The first slight swerving of the heart,
　　That words are powerless to express,

And leave it still unsaid in part,
    Or say it in too great excess.

The very tones in which we spake
    Had something strange, I could but mark;
The leaves of memory seemed to make
    A mournful rustling in the dark.

Oft died the words upon our lips,
    As suddenly, from out the fire
Built of the wreck of stranded ships,
    The flames would leap and then expire.

And, as their splendor flashed and failed,
    We thought of wrecks upon the main,
Of ships dismasted, that were hailed
    And sent no answer back again.

The windows, rattling in their frames,
    The ocean, roaring up the beach,
The gusty blast, the bickering flames,
    All mingled vaguely in our speech;

Until they made themselves a part
    Of fancies floating through the brain,
The long-lost ventures of the heart,
    That send no answers back again.

O flames that glowed! O hearts that yearned!
    They were indeed too much akin,
The drift-wood fire without that burned,
    The thoughts that burned and glowed within.

The Building of the Ship

"Build me straight, O worthy Master!
 Stanch and strong, a goodly vessel,
That shall laugh at all disaster,
 And with wave and whirlwind wrestle!"

The merchant's word
Delighted the Master heard;
For his heart was in his work, and the heart
Giveth grace unto every Art.
A quiet smile played round his lips,
As the eddies and dimples of the tide
Play round the bows of ships,
That steadily at anchor ride.
And with a voice that was full of glee,
He answered, "Erelong we will launch
A vessel as goodly, and strong, and stanch,
As ever weathered a wintry sea!"
And first with nicest skill and art,
Perfect and finished in every part,
A little model the Master wrought,
Which should be to the larger plan
What the child is to the man,
Its counterpart in miniature;
That with a hand more swift and sure
The greater labor might be brought
To answer to his inward thought.
And as he labored, his mind ran o'er
The various ships that were built of yore,
And above them all, and strangest of all
Towered the Great Harry, crank and tall,

Whose picture was hanging on the wall,
With bows and stern raised high in air,
And balconies hanging here and there,
And signal lanterns and flags afloat,
And eight round towers, like those that frown
From some old castle, looking down
Upon the drawbridge and the moat.
And he said with a smile, "Our ship, I wis,
Shall be of another form than this!"
It was of another form, indeed;
Built for freight, and yet for speed,
A beautiful and gallant craft;
Broad in the beam, that the stress of the blast,
Pressing down upon sail and mast,
Might not the sharp bows overwhelm;
Broad in the beam, but sloping aft
With graceful curve and slow degrees,
That she might be docile to the helm,
And that the currents of parted seas,
Closing behind, with mighty force,
Might aid and not impede her course.

In the ship-yard stood the Master,
With the model of the vessel,
That should laugh at all disaster,
And with wave and whirlwind wrestle!
Covering many a rood of ground,
Lay the timber piled around;
Timber of chestnut, and elm, and oak,
And scattered here and there, with these,
The knarred and crooked cedar knees;
Brought from regions far away,

From Pascagoula's sunny bay,
And the banks of the roaring Roanoke!
Ah! what a wondrous thing it is
To note how many wheels of toil
One thought, one word, can set in motion!
There's not a ship that sails the ocean,
But every climate, every soil,
Must bring its tribute, great or small,
And help to build the wooden wall!

The sun was rising o'er the sea,
And long the level shadows lay,
As if they, too, the beams would be
Of some great, airy argosy,
Framed and launched in a single day.
That silent architect, the sun,
Had hewn and laid them every one,
Ere the work of man was yet begun.
Beside the Master, when he spoke,
A youth, against an anchor leaning,
Listened, to catch his slightest meaning.
Only the long waves, as they broke
In ripples on the pebbly beach,
Interrupted the old man's speech.
Beautiful they were, in sooth,
The old man and the fiery youth!
The old man, in whose busy brain
Many a ship that sailed the main
Was modelled o'er and o'er again;—
The fiery youth, who was to be
The heir of his dexterity,
The heir of his house, and his daughter's hand,

When he had built and launched from land
What the elder head had planned.

"Thus," said he, "will we build this ship!
Lay square the blocks upon the slip,
And follow well this plan of mine.
Choose the timbers with greatest care;
Of all that is unsound beware;
For only what is sound and strong
To this vessel shall belong.
Cedar of Maine and Georgia pine
Here together shall combine.
A goodly frame, and a goodly fame,
And the UNION be her name!
For the day that gives her to the sea
Shall give my daughter unto thee!"

The Master's word
Enraptured the young man heard;
And as he turned his face aside,
With a look of joy and a thrill of pride
Standing before
Her father's door,
He saw the form of his promised bride.
The sun shone on her golden hair,
And her cheek was glowing fresh and fair,
With the breath of morn and the soft sea air.
Like a beauteous barge was she,
Still at rest on the sandy beach,
Just beyond the billow's reach;
But he
Was the restless, seething, stormy sea!

Ah, how skilful grows the hand
That obeyeth Love's command!
It is the heart, and not the brain,
That to the highest doth attain,
And he who followeth Love's behest
Far excelleth all the rest!

Thus with the rising of the sun
        Was the noble task begun,
And soon throughout the ship-yard's bounds
Were heard the intermingled sounds
Of axes and of mallets, plied
With vigorous arms on every side;
Plied so deftly and so well,
That, ere the shadows of evening fell,
The keel of oak for a noble ship,
Scarfed and bolted, straight and strong,
Was lying ready, and stretched along
The blocks, well placed upon the slip.
Happy, thrice happy, every one
Who sees his labor well begun,
And not perplexed and multiplied,
By idly waiting for time and tide!

And when the hot, long day was o'er,
The young man at the Master's door
Sat with the maiden calm and still,
And within the porch, a little more
Removed beyond the evening chill,
The father sat, and told them tales
Of wrecks in the great September gales,
Of pirates coasting the Spanish Main,

And ships that never came back again,
The chance and change of a sailor's life,
Want and plenty, rest and strife,
His roving fancy, like the wind,
That nothing can stay and nothing can bind,
And the magic charm of foreign lands,
With shadows of palms, and shining sands,
Where the tumbling surf,
O'er the coral reefs of Madagascar,
Washes the feet of the swarthy Lascar,
As he lies alone and asleep on the turf.
And the trembling maiden held her breath
At the tales of that awful, pitiless sea,
With all its terror and mystery,
The dim, dark sea, so like unto Death,
That divides and yet unites mankind!
And whenever the old man paused, a gleam
From the bowl of his pipe would awhile illume
The silent group in the twilight gloom,
And thoughtful faces, as in a dream;
And for a moment one might mark
What had been hidden by the dark,
That the head of the maiden lay at rest,
Tenderly, on the young man's breast!

Day by day the vessel grew,
With timbers fashioned strong and true,
Stemson and keelson and sternson-knee,
Till, framed with perfect symmetry,
A skeleton ship rose up to view!
And around the bows and along the side
The heavy hammers and mallets plied,

Till after many a week, at length,
Wonderful for form and strength,
Sublime in its enormous bulk,
Loomed aloft the shadowy hulk!
And around it columns of smoke, upwreathing,
Rose from the boiling, bubbling, seething
Caldron, that glowed,
And overflowed
With the black tar, heated for the sheathing.
And amid the clamors
Of clattering hammers,
He who listened heard now and then
The song of the Master and his men:—

"Build me straight, O worthy Master,
    Staunch and strong, a goodly vessel,
That shall laugh at all disaster,
    And with wave and whirlwind wrestle!"

With oaken brace and copper band,
Lay the rudder on the sand,
That, like a thought, should have control
Over the movement of the whole;
And near it the anchor, whose giant hand
Would reach down and grapple with the land,
And immovable and fast
Hold the great ship against the bellowing blast!
And at the bows an image stood,
By a cunning artist carved in wood,
With robes of white, that far behind
Seemed to be fluttering in the wind.
It was not shaped in a classic mould,

Not like a Nymph or Goddess of old,
Or Naiad rising from the water,
But modelled from the Master's daughter!
On many a dreary and misty night,
'Twill be seen by the rays of the signal light,
Speeding along through the rain and the dark,
Like a ghost in its snow-white sark,
The pilot of some phantom bark,
Guiding the vessel, in its flight,
By a path none other knows aright!

Behold, at last,
Each tall and tapering mast
Is swung into its place;
Shrouds and stays
Holding it firm and fast!

Long ago,
In the deer-haunted forests of Maine,
When upon mountain and plain
Lay the snow,
They fell,—those lordly pines!
Those grand, majestic pines!
'Mid shouts and cheers
The jaded steers,
Panting beneath the goad,
Dragged down the weary, winding road
Those captive kings so straight and tall,
To be shorn of their streaming hair,
And naked and bare,
To feel the stress and the strain
Of the wind and the reeling main,

Whose roar
Would remind them forevermore
Of their native forests they should not see again.
And everywhere
The slender, graceful spars
Poise aloft in the air,
And at the mast-head,
White, blue, and red,
A flag unrolls the stripes and stars.
Ah! when the wanderer, lonely, friendless,
In foreign harbors shall behold
That flag unrolled,
'Twill be as a friendly hand
Stretched out from his native land,
Filling his heart with memories sweet and endless!

All is finished! and at length
Has come the bridal day
Of beauty and of strength.
To-day the vessel shall be launched!
With fleecy clouds the sky is blanched,
And o'er the bay,
Slowly, in all his splendors dight,
The great sun rises to behold the sight.

The ocean old,
Centuries old,
Strong as youth, and as uncontrolled,
Paces restless to and fro,
Up and down the sands of gold.
His beating heart is not at rest;
And far and wide,

With ceaseless flow,
His beard of snow
Heaves with the heaving of his breast.
He waits impatient for his bride.
There she stands,
With her foot upon the sands,
Decked with flags and streamers gay,
In honor of her marriage day,
Her snow-white signals fluttering, blending,
Round her like a veil descending,
Ready to be
The bride of the gray old sea.

On the deck another bride
Is standing by her lover's side.
Shadows from the flags and shrouds,
Like the shadows cast by clouds,
Broken by many a sudden fleck,
Fall around them on the deck.

The prayer is said,
The service read,
The joyous bridegroom bows his head;
And in tears the good old Master
Shakes the brown hand of his son,
Kisses his daughter's glowing cheek
In silence, for he cannot speak,
And ever faster
Down his own the tears begin to run.
The worthy pastor—
The shepherd of that wandering flock,
That has the ocean for its wold,

That has the vessel for its fold,
Leaping ever from rock to rock—
Spake, with accents mild and clear,
Words of warning, words of cheer,
But tedious to the bridegroom's ear.
He knew the chart
Of the sailor's heart,
All its pleasures and its griefs,
All its shallows and rocky reefs,
All those secret currents, that flow
With such resistless undertow,
And lift and drift, with terrible force,
The will from its moorings and its course.
Therefore he spake, and thus said he:—

"Like unto ships far off at sea,
Outward or homeward bound, are we.
Before, behind, and all around,
Floats and swings the horizon's bound,
Seems at its distant rim to rise
And climb the crystal wall of the skies,
And then again to turn and sink,
As if we could slide from its outer brink.
Ah! it is not the sea,
It is not the sea that sinks and shelves,
But ourselves
That rock and rise
With endless and uneasy motion,
Now touching the very skies,
Now sinking into the depths of ocean.
Ah! if our souls but poise and swing
Like the compass in its brazen ring,

Ever level and ever true
To the toil and the task we have to do,
We shall sail securely, and safely reach
The Fortunate Isles, on whose shining beach
The sights we see, and the sounds we hear,
Will be those of joy and not of fear!"

Then the Master,
With a gesture of command,
Waved his hand;
And at the word,
Loud and sudden there was heard,
All around them and below,
The sound of hammers, blow on blow,
Knocking away the shores and spurs.
And see! she stirs!
She starts,—she moves,—she seems to feel
The thrill of life along her keel,
And, spurning with her foot the ground,
With one exulting, joyous bound,
She leaps into the ocean's arms!

And lo! from the assembled crowd
There rose a shout, prolonged and loud,
That to the ocean seemed to say,
"Take her, O bridegroom, old and gray,
Take her to thy protecting arms,
With all her youth and all her charms!"

How beautiful she is! How fair
She lies within those arms, that press
Her form with many a soft caress

Of tenderness and watchful care!
Sail forth into the sea, O ship!
Through wind and wave, right onward steer!
The moistened eye, the trembling lip,
Are not the signs of doubt or fear.
Sail forth into the sea of life,
O gentle, loving, trusting wife,
And safe from all adversity
Upon the bosom of that sea
Thy comings and thy goings be!
For gentleness and love and trust
Prevail o'er angry wave and gust;
And in the wreck of noble lives
Something immortal still survives!

Thou, too, sail on, O Ship of State!
Sail on, O UNION, strong and great!
Humanity with all its fears,
With all the hopes of future years,
Is hanging breathless on thy fate!
We know what Master laid thy keel,
What Workmen wrought thy ribs of steel,
Who made each mast, and sail, and rope,
What anvils rang, what hammers beat,
In what a forge and what a heat
Were shaped the anchors of thy hope!
Fear not each sudden sound and shock,
'Tis of the wave and not the rock;
'Tis but the flapping of the sail,
And not a rent made by the gale!
In spite of rock and tempest's roar,
In spite of false lights on the shore,

Sail on, nor fear to breast the sea!
Our hearts, our hopes, are all with thee,
Our hearts, our hopes, our prayers, our tears,
Our faith triumphant o'er our fears,
Are all with thee,—are all with thee!

Seaweed

When descends on the Atlantic
    The gigantic
Storm-wind of the equinox,
Landward in his wrath he scourges
    The toiling surges,
Laden with seaweed from the rocks:

From Bermuda's reefs; from edges
    Of sunken ledges,
In some far-off, bright Azore;
From Bahama, and the dashing,
    Silver-flashing
Surges of San Salvador;

From the tumbling surf, that buries
    The Orkneyan skerries,
Answering the hoarse Hebrides;
And from wrecks of ships, and drifting
    Spars, uplifting
On the desolate, rainy seas;—

Ever drifting, drifting, drifting
    On the shifting
Currents of the restless main;
Till in sheltered coves, and reaches
    Of sandy beaches,
All have found repose again.

So when storms of wild emotion
    Strike the ocean

Of the poet's soul, erelong
From each cave and rocky fastness,
    In its vastness,
Floats some fragment of a song:

From the far-off isles enchanted,
    Heaven has planted
With the golden fruit of Truth;
From the flashing surf, whose vision
    Gleams Elysian
In the tropic clime of Youth;

From the strong Will, and the Endeavor
    That forever
Wrestle with the tides of Fate;
From the wreck of Hopes far-scattered,
    Tempest-shattered,
Floating waste and desolate;—

Ever drifting, drifting, drifting
    On the shifting
Currents of the restless heart;
Till at length in books recorded,
    They, like hoarded
Household words, no more depart.

The Secret of the Sea

Ah! what pleasant visions haunt me
    As I gaze upon the sea!
All the old romantic legends,
    All my dreams, come back to me.

Sails of silk and ropes of sandal,
    Such as gleam in ancient lore;
And the singing of the sailors,
    And the answer from the shore!

Most of all, the Spanish ballad
    Haunts me oft, and tarries long,
Of the noble Count Arnaldos
    And the sailor's mystic song.

Like the long waves on a sea-beach,
    Where the sand as silver shines,
With a soft, monotonous cadence,
    Flow its unrhymed lyric lines:—

Telling how the Count Arnaldos,
    With his hawk upon his hand,
Saw a fair and stately galley,
    Steering onward to the land;—

How he heard the ancient helmsman
    Chant a song so wild and clear,
That the sailing sea-bird slowly
    Poised upon the mast to hear,

Till his soul was full of longing,
          And he cried, with impulse strong,—
"Helmsman! for the love of heaven,
          Teach me, too, that wondrous song!"

"Wouldst thou,"—so the helmsman answered,
          "Learn the secret of the sea?
Only those who brave its dangers
          Comprehend its mystery!"

In each sail that skims the horizon,
          In each landward-blowing breeze,
I behold that stately galley,
          Hear those mournful melodies;

Till my soul is full of longing
          For the secret of the sea,
And the heart of the great ocean
          Sends a thrilling pulse through me.

The Jewish Cemetery at Newport

How strange it seems! These Hebrews in their graves,
    Close by the street of this fair seaport town,
Silent beside the never-silent waves,
    At rest in all this moving up and down!

The trees are white with dust, that o'er their sleep
    Wave their broad curtains in the south-wind's breath,
While underneath such leafy tents they keep
    The long, mysterious Exodus of Death.

And these sepulchral stones, so old and brown,
    That pave with level flags their burial-place,
Seem like the tablets of the Law, thrown down
    And broken by Moses at the mountain's base.

The very names recorded here are strange,
    Of foreign accent, and of different climes;
Alvares and Rivera interchange
    With Abraham and Jacob of old times.

"Blessed be God! for he created Death!"
    The mourners said, "and Death is rest and peace;"
Then added, in the certainty of faith,
    "And giveth Life that never more shall cease."

Closed are the portals of their Synagogue,
    No Psalms of David now the silence break,
No Rabbi reads the ancient Decalogue
    In the grand dialect the Prophets spake.

Gone are the living, but the dead remain,
    And not neglected; for a hand unseen,
Scattering its bounty, like a summer rain,
    Still keeps their graves and their remembrance green.

How came they here? What burst of Christian hate,
    What persecution, merciless and blind,
Drove o'er the sea—that desert desolate—
    These Ishmaels and Hagars of mankind?

They lived in narrow streets and lanes obscure,
    Ghetto and Judenstrass, in mirk and mire;
Taught in the school of patience to endure
    The life of anguish and the death of fire.

All their lives long, with the unleavened bread
    And bitter herbs of exile and its fears,
The wasting famine of the heart they fed,
    And slaked its thirst with marah of their tears.

Anathema maranatha! was the cry
    That rang from town to town, from street to street;
At every gate the accursed Mordecai
    Was mocked and jeered, and spurned by Christian
        feet.

Pride and humiliation hand in hand
        Walked with them through the world where'er they
        went;
Trampled and beaten were they as the sand,
    And yet unshaken as the continent.

For in the background figures vague and vast
    Of patriarchs and of prophets rose sublime,
And all the great traditions of the Past
    They saw reflected in the coming time.

And thus for ever with reverted look
    The mystic volume of the world they read,
Spelling it backward, like a Hebrew book,
    Till life became a Legend of the Dead.

But ah! what once has been shall be no more!
    The groaning earth in travail and in pain
Brings forth its races, but does not restore,
    And the dead nations never rise again.

Hiawatha's Wooing (from *The Song of Hiawatha*)

"As unto the bow the cord is,
So unto the man is woman;
Though she bends him, she obeys him,
Though she draws him, yet she follows;
Useless each without the other!"
        Thus the youthful Hiawatha
Said within himself and pondered,
Much perplexed by various feelings,
Listless, longing, hoping, fearing,
Dreaming still of Minnehaha,
Of the lovely Laughing Water,
In the land of the Dacotahs.
        "Wed a maiden of your people,"
Warning said the old Nokomis;
"Go not eastward, go not westward,
For a stranger, whom we know not!
Like a fire upon the hearth-stone
Is a neighbor's homely daughter,
Like the starlight or the moonlight
Is the handsomest of strangers!"
        Thus dissuading spake Nokomis,
And my Hiawatha answered
Only this: "Dear old Nokomis,
Very pleasant is the firelight,
But I like the starlight better,
Better do I like the moonlight!"
        Gravely then said old Nokomis:
"Bring not here an idle maiden,
Bring not here a useless woman,
Hands unskilful, feet unwilling;

Bring a wife with nimble fingers,
Heart and hand that move together,
Feet that run on willing errands!"

Smiling answered Hiawatha:
"In the land of the Dacotahs
Lives the Arrow-maker's daughter,
Minnehaha, Laughing Water,
Handsomest of all the women.
I will bring her to your wigwam,
She shall run upon your errands,
Be your starlight, moonlight, firelight,
Be the sunlight of my people!"

Still dissuading said Nokomis:
"Bring not to my lodge a stranger
From the land of the Dacotahs!
Very fierce are the Dacotahs,
Often is there war between us,
There are feuds yet unforgotten,
Wounds that ache and still may open!"

Laughing answered Hiawatha:
"For that reason, if no other,
Would I wed the fair Dacotah,
That our tribes might be united,
That old feuds might be forgotten,
And old wounds be healed forever!"

Thus departed Hiawatha
To the land of the Dacotahs,
To the land of handsome women;
Striding over moor and meadow,
Through interminable forests,
Through uninterrupted silence.

With his moccasins of magic,

At each stride a mile he measured;
Yet the way seemed long before him,
And his heart outran his footsteps;
And he journeyed without resting,
Till he heard the cataract's laughter,
Heard the Falls of Minnehaha
Calling to him through the silence.
"Pleasant is the sound!" he murmured,
"Pleasant is the voice that calls me!"

On the outskirts of the forests,
'Twixt the shadow and the sunshine,
Herds of fallow deer were feeding,
But they saw not Hiawatha;
To his bow he whispered, "Fail not!"
To his arrow whispered, "Swerve not!"
Sent it singing on its errand,
To the red heart of the roebuck;
Threw the deer across his shoulder,
And sped forward without pausing.

At the doorway of his wigwam
Sat the ancient Arrow-maker,
In the land of the Dacotahs,
Making arrow-heads of jasper,
Arrow-heads of chalcedony.
At his side, in all her beauty,
Sat the lovely Minnehaha,
Sat his daughter, Laughing Water,
Plaiting mats of flags and rushes;
Of the past the old man's thoughts were,
And the maiden's of the future.

He was thinking, as he sat there,
Of the days when with such arrows

He had struck the deer and bison,
On the Muskoday, the meadow;
Shot the wild goose, flying southward
On the wing, the clamorous Wawa;
Thinking of the great war-parties,
How they came to buy his arrows,
Could not fight without his arrows.
Ah, no more such noble warriors
Could be found on earth as they were!
Now the men were all like women,
Only used their tongues for weapons!

She was thinking of a hunter,
From another tribe and country,
Young and tall and very handsome,
Who one morning, in the Spring-time,
Came to buy her father's arrows,
Sat and rested in the wigwam,
Lingered long about the doorway,
Looking back as he departed.
She had heard her father praise him,
Praise his courage and his wisdom;
Would he come again for arrows
To the Falls of Minnehaha?
On the mat her hands lay idle,
And her eyes were very dreamy.

Through their thoughts they heard a footstep,
Heard a rustling in the branches,
And with glowing cheek and forehead,
With the deer upon his shoulders,
Suddenly from out the woodlands
Hiawatha stood before them.

Straight the ancient Arrow-maker

Looked up gravely from his labor,
Laid aside the unfinished arrow,
Bade him enter at the doorway,
Saying, as he rose to meet him,
"Hiawatha, you are welcome!"

At the feet of Laughing Water
Hiawatha laid his burden,
Threw the red deer from his shoulders;
And the maiden looked up at him,
Looked up from her mat of rushes,
Said with gentle look and accent,
"You are welcome, Hiawatha!"

Very spacious was the wigwam,
Made of deer-skins dressed and whitened,
With the Gods of the Dacotahs
Drawn and painted on its curtains,
And so tall the doorway, hardly
Hiawatha stooped to enter,
Hardly touched his eagle-feathers
As he entered at the doorway.

Then uprose the Laughing Water,
From the ground fair Minnehaha,
Laid aside her mat unfinished,
Brought forth food and set before them,
Water brought them from the brooklet,
Gave them food in earthen vessels,
Gave them drink in bowls of bass-wood,
Listened while the guest was speaking,
Listened while her father answered,
But not once her lips she opened,
Not a single word she uttered.

Yes, as in a dream she listened

To the words of Hiawatha,
As he talked of old Nokomis,
Who had nursed him in his childhood,
As he told of his companions,
Chibiabos, the musician,
And the very strong man, Kwasind,
And of happiness and plenty
In the land of the Ojibways,
In the pleasant land and peaceful.

"After many years of warfare,
Many years of strife and bloodshed,
There is peace between the Ojibways
And the tribe of the Dacotahs."
Thus continued Hiawatha,
And then added, speaking slowly,
"That this peace may last forever,
And our hands be clasped more closely,
And our hearts be more united,
Give me as my wife this maiden,
Minnehaha, Laughing Water,
Loveliest of Dacotah women!"

And the ancient Arrow-maker
Paused a moment ere he answered,
Smoked a little while in silence,
Looked at Hiawatha proudly,
Fondly looked at Laughing Water,
And made answer very gravely:
"Yes, if Minnehaha wishes;
Let your heart speak, Minnehaha!"

And the lovely Laughing Water
Seemed more lovely as she stood there,
Neither willing nor reluctant,

As she went to Hiawatha,
Softly took the seat beside him,
While she said, and blushed to say it,
"I will follow you, my husband!"

This was Hiawatha's wooing!
Thus it was he won the daughter
Of the ancient Arrow-maker,
In the land of the Dacotahs!

From the wigwam he departed,
Leading with him Laughing Water;
Hand in hand they went together,
Through the woodland and the meadow,
Left the old man standing lonely
At the doorway of his wigwam,
Heard the Falls of Minnehaha
Calling to them from the distance,
Crying to them from afar off,
"Fare thee well, O Minnehaha!"

And the ancient Arrow-maker
Turned again unto his labor,
Sat down by his sunny doorway,
Murmuring to himself, and saying:
"Thus it is our daughters leave us,
Those we love, and those who love us!
Just when they have learned to help us,
When we are old and lean upon them,
Comes a youth with flaunting feathers,
With his flute of reeds, a stranger
Wanders piping through the village,
Beckons to the fairest maiden,
And she follows where he leads her,
Leaving all things for the stranger!"

Pleasant was the journey homeward,
Through interminable forests,
Over meadow, over mountain,
Over river, hill, and hollow.
Short it seemed to Hiawatha,
Though they journeyed very slowly,
Though his pace he checked and slackened
To the steps of Laughing Water.

Over wide and rushing rivers
In his arms he bore the maiden;
Light he thought her as a feather,
As the plume upon his head-gear;
Cleared the tangled pathway for her,
Bent aside the swaying branches,
Made at night a lodge of branches,
And a bed with boughs of hemlock,
And a fire before the doorway
With the dry cones of the pine-tree.

All the travelling winds went with them,
O'er the meadows, through the forest;
All the stars of night looked at them,
Watched with sleepless eyes their slumber;
From his ambush in the oak-tree
Peeped the squirrel, Adjidaumo,
Watched with eager eyes the lovers;
And the rabbit, the Wabasso,
Scampered from the path before them,
Peering, peeping from his burrow,
Sat erect upon his haunches,
Watched with curious eyes the lovers.

Pleasant was the journey homeward!
All the birds sang loud and sweetly

Songs of happiness and heart's-ease;
Sang the bluebird, the Owaissa,
"Happy are you, Hiawatha,
Having such a wife to love you!"
Sang the robin, the Opechee,
"Happy are you, Laughing Water,
Having such a noble husband!"

From the sky the sun benignant
Looked upon them through the branches,
Saying to them, "O my children,
Love is sunshine, hate is shadow,
Life is checkered shade and sunshine,
Rule by love, O Hiawatha!"

From the sky the moon looked at them,
Filled the lodge with mystic splendors,
Whispered to them, "O my children,
Day is restless, night is quiet,
Man imperious, woman feeble;
Half is mine, although I follow;
Rule by patience, Laughing Water!"

Thus it was they journeyed homeward;
Thus it was that Hiawatha
To the lodge of old Nokomis
Brought the moonlight, starlight, firelight,
Brought the sunshine of his people,
Minnehaha, Laughing Water,
Handsomest of all the women
In the land of the Dacotahs,
In the land of handsome women.

The Famine (from *The Song of Hiawatha*)

Oh the long and dreary Winter!
Oh the cold and cruel Winter!
Ever thicker, thicker, thicker
Froze the ice on lake and river,
Ever deeper, deeper, deeper
Fell the snow o'er all the landscape,
Fell the covering snow, and drifted
Through the forest, round the village.

 Hardly from his buried wigwam
Could the hunter force a passage;
With his mittens and his snow-shoes
Vainly walked he through the forest,
Sought for bird or beast and found none,
Saw no track of deer or rabbit,
In the snow beheld no footprints,
In the ghastly, gleaming forest
Fell, and could not rise from weakness,
Perished there from cold and hunger.

 Oh the famine and the fever!
Oh the wasting of the famine!
Oh the blasting of the fever!
Oh the wailing of the children!
Oh the anguish of the women!

 All the earth was sick and famished;
Hungry was the air around them,
Hungry was the sky above them,
And the hungry stars in heaven
Like the eyes of wolves glared at them!

 Into Hiawatha's wigwam
Came two other guests, as silent

As the ghosts were, and as gloomy,
Waited not to be invited,
Did not parley at the doorway,
Sat there without word of welcome
In the seat of Laughing Water;
Looked with haggard eyes and hollow
At the face of Laughing Water.

And the foremost said: "Behold me!
I am Famine, Bukadawin!"
And the other said: "Behold me!
I am Fever, Ahkosewin!"

And the lovely Minnehaha
Shuddered as they looked upon her,
Shuddered at the words they uttered,
Lay down on her bed in silence,
Hid her face, but made no answer;
Lay there trembling, freezing, burning
At the looks they cast upon her,
At the fearful words they uttered.

Forth into the empty forest
Rushed the maddened Hiawatha;
In his heart was deadly sorrow,
In his face a stony firmness;
On his brow the sweat of anguish
Started, but it froze and fell not.

Wrapped in furs and armed for hunting,
With his mighty bow of ash-tree,
With his quiver full of arrows,
With his mittens, Minjekahwun,
Into the vast and vacant forest
On his snow-shoes strode he forward.

"Gitche Manito, the Mighty!"

Cried he with his face uplifted
In that bitter hour of anguish,
"Give your children food, O father!
Give us food, or we must perish!
Give me food for Minnehaha,
For my dying Minnehaha!"

Through the far-resounding forest,
Through the forest vast and vacant
Rang that cry of desolation,
But there came no other answer
Than the echo of his crying,
Than the echo of the woodlands,
"Minnehaha! Minnehaha!"

All day long roved Hiawatha
In that melancholy forest,
Through the shadow of whose thickets,
In the pleasant days of Summer,
Of that ne'er forgotten Summer,
He had brought his young wife homeward
From the land of the Dacotahs;
When the birds sang in the thickets,
And the streamlets laughed and glistened,
And the air was full of fragrance,
And the lovely Laughing Water
Said with voice that did not tremble,
"I will follow you, my husband!"

In the wigwam with Nokomis,
With those gloomy guests that watched her,
With the Famine and the Fever,
She was lying, the Beloved,
She, the dying Minnehaha.

"Hark!" she said; "I hear a rushing,

Hear a roaring and a rushing,
Hear the Falls of Minnehaha
Calling to me from a distance!"
"No, my child!" said old Nokomis,
"'Tis the night-wind in the pine-trees!"

    "Look!" she said; "I see my father
Standing lonely at his doorway,
Beckoning to me from his wigwam
In the land of the Dacotahs!"
"No, my child!" said old Nokomis.
"'Tis the smoke, that waves and beckons!"

    "Ah!" said she, "the eyes of Pauguk
Glare upon me in the darkness,
I can feel his icy fingers
Clasping mine amid the darkness!
Hiawatha! Hiawatha!"

    And the desolate Hiawatha,
Far away amid the forest,
Miles away among the mountains,
Heard that sudden cry of anguish,
Heard the voice of Minnehaha
Calling to him in the darkness,
"Hiawatha! Hiawatha!"

    Over snow-fields waste and pathless,
Under snow-encumbered branches,
Homeward hurried Hiawatha,
Empty-handed, heavy-hearted,
Heard Nokomis moaning, wailing:
"Wahonowin! Wahonowin!
Would that I had perished for you,
Would that I were dead as you are!
Wahonowin! Wahonowin!"

And he rushed into the wigwam,
Saw the old Nokomis slowly
Rocking to and fro and moaning,
Saw his lovely Minnehaha
Lying dead and cold before him,
And his bursting heart within him
Uttered such a cry of anguish,
That the forest moaned and shuddered,
That the very stars in heaven
Shook and trembled with his anguish.

Then he sat down, still and speechless,
On the bed of Minnehaha,
At the feet of Laughing Water,
At those willing feet, that never
More would lightly run to meet him,
Never more would lightly follow.

With both hands his face he covered,
Seven long days and nights he sat there,
As if in a swoon he sat there,
Speechless, motionless, unconscious
Of the daylight or the darkness.

Then they buried Minnehaha;
In the snow a grave they made her,
In the forest deep and darksome,
Underneath the moaning hemlocks;
Clothed her in her richest garments,
Wrapped her in her robes of ermine,
Covered her with snow, like ermine;
Thus they buried Minnehaha.

And at night a fire was lighted,
On her grave four times was kindled,
For her soul upon its journey

To the Islands of the Blessed.
From his doorway Hiawatha
Saw it burning in the forest,
Lighting up the gloomy hemlocks;
From his sleepless bed uprising,
From the bed of Minnehaha,
Stood and watched it at the doorway,
That it might not be extinguished,
Might not leave her in the darkness.

    "Farewell!" said he, "Minnehaha!
Farewell, O my Laughing Water!
All my heart is buried with you,
All my thoughts go onward with you!
Come not back again to labor,
Come not back again to suffer,
Where the Famine and the Fever
Wear the heart and waste the body.
Soon my task will be completed,
Soon your footsteps I shall follow
To the Islands of the Blessed,
To the Kingdom of Ponemah,
To the Land of the Hereafter!"

Hiawatha's Departure (from *The Song of Hiawatha*)

By the shore of Gitche Gumee,
By the shining Big-Sea-Water,
At the doorway of his wigwam,
In the pleasant Summer morning,
Hiawatha stood and waited.
All the air was full of freshness,
All the earth was bright and joyous,
And before him, through the sunshine,
Westward toward the neighboring forest
Passed in golden swarms the Ahmo,
Passed the bees, the honey-makers,
Burning, singing in the sunshine.

Bright above him shone the heavens,
Level spread the lake before him;
From its bosom leaped the sturgeon,
Sparkling, flashing in the sunshine;
On its margin the great forest
Stood reflected in the water,
Every tree-top had its shadow,
Motionless beneath the water.

From the brow of Hiawatha
Gone was every trace of sorrow,
As the fog from off the water,
As the mist from off the meadow.
With a smile of joy and triumph,
With a look of exultation,
As of one who in a vision
Sees what is to be, but is not,
Stood and waited Hiawatha.

Toward the sun his hands were lifted,

Both the palms spread out against it,
And between the parted fingers
Fell the sunshine on his features,
Flecked with light his naked shoulders,
As it falls and flecks an oak-tree
Through the rifted leaves and branches.

O'er the water floating, flying,
Something in the hazy distance,
Something in the mists of morning,
Loomed and lifted from the water,
Now seemed floating, now seemed flying,
Coming nearer, nearer, nearer.

Was it Shingebis the diver?
Or the pelican, the Shada?
Or the heron, the Shuh-shuh-gah?
Or the white goose, Waw-be-wawa,
With the water dripping, flashing,
From its glossy neck and feathers?

It was neither goose nor diver,
Neither pelican nor heron,
O'er the water floating, flying,
Through the shining mist of morning,
But a birch canoe with paddles,
Rising, sinking on the water,
Dripping, flashing in the sunshine;
And within it came a people
From the distant land of Wabun,
From the farthest realms of morning
Came the Black-Robe chief, the Prophet,
He the Priest of Prayer, the Pale-face,
With his guides and his companions.

And the noble Hiawatha,

With his hands aloft extended,
Held aloft in sign of welcome,
Waited, full of exultation,
Till the birch canoe with paddles
Grated on the shining pebbles,
Stranded on the sandy margin,
Till the Black-Robe chief, the Pale-face,
With the cross upon his bosom,
Landed on the sandy margin.

    Then the joyous Hiawatha
Cried aloud and spake in this wise:
"Beautiful is the sun, O strangers,
When you come so far to see us!
All our town in peace awaits you,
All our doors stand open for you;
You shall enter all our wigwams,
For the heart's right hand we give you.

    "Never bloomed the earth so gayly,
Never shone the sun so brightly,
As to-day they shine and blossom
When you come so far to see us!
Never was our lake so tranquil,
Nor so free from rocks and sand-bars;
For your birch canoe in passing
Has removed both rock and sand-bar.

    "Never before had our tobacco
Such a sweet and pleasant flavor,
Never the broad leaves of our cornfields
Were so beautiful to look on,
As they seem to us this morning,
When you come so far to see us!"

    And the Black-Robe chief made answer,

Stammered in his speech a little,
Speaking words yet unfamiliar:
"Peace be with you, Hiawatha,
Peace be with you and your people,
Peace of prayer, and peace of pardon,
Peace of Christ, and joy of Mary!"

Then the generous Hiawatha
Led the strangers to his wigwam,
Seated them on skins of bison,
Seated them on skins of ermine,
And the careful old Nokomis
Brought them food in bowls of basswood,
Water brought in birchen dippers,
And the calumet, the peace-pipe,
Filled and lighted for their smoking.

All the old men of the village,
All the warriors of the nation,
All the Jossakeeds, the Prophets,
The magicians, the Wabenos,
And the Medicine-men, the Medas,
Came to bid the strangers welcome;
"It is well," they said, "O brothers,
That you come so far to see us!"

In a circle round the doorway,
With their pipes they sat in silence,
Waiting to behold the strangers,
Waiting to receive their message;
Till the Black-Robe chief, the Pale-face,
From the wigwam came to greet them,
Stammering in his speech a little,
Speaking words yet unfamiliar;
"It is well," they said, "O brother,

That you come so far to see us!"
Then the Black-Robe chief, the Prophet,
Told his message to the people,
Told the purport of his mission,
Told them of the Virgin Mary,
And her blessed Son, the Saviour,
How in distant lands and ages
He had lived on earth as we do;
How he fasted, prayed, and labored;
How the Jews, the tribe accursed,
Mocked him, scourged him, crucified him;
How he rose from where they laid him,
Walked again with his disciples,
And ascended into heaven.

And the chiefs made answer, saying:
"We have listened to your message,
We have heard your words of wisdom,
We will think on what you tell us.
It is well for us, O brothers,
That you come so far to see us!"

Then they rose up and departed
Each one homeward to his wigwam,
To the young men and the women
Told the story of the strangers
Whom the Master of Life had sent them
From the shining land of Wabun.

Heavy with the heat and silence
Grew the afternoon of Summer;
With a drowsy sound the forest
Whispered round the sultry wigwam,
With a sound of sleep the water
Rippled on the beach below it;

From the cornfields shrill and ceaseless
Sang the grasshopper, Pah-puk-keena;
And the guests of Hiawatha,
Weary with the heat of Summer,
Slumbered in the sultry wigwam.

Slowly o'er the simmering landscape
Fell the evening's dusk and coolness,
And the long and level sunbeams
Shot their spears into the forest,
Breaking through its shields of shadow,
Rushed into each secret ambush,
Searched each thicket, dingle, hollow;
Still the guests of Hiawatha
Slumbered in the silent wigwam.

From his place rose Hiawatha,
Bade farewell to old Nokomis,
Spake in whispers, spake in this wise,
Did not wake the guests, that slumbered:

"I am going, O Nokomis,
On a long and distant journey,
To the portals of the Sunset,
To the regions of the home-wind,
Of the Northwest-Wind, Keewaydin.
But these guests I leave behind me,
In your watch and ward I leave them;
See that never harm comes near them,
See that never fear molests them,
Never danger nor suspicion,
Never want of food or shelter,
In the lodge of Hiawatha!"

Forth into the village went he,
Bade farewell to all the warriors,

Bade farewell to all the young men,
Spake persuading, spake in this wise:

"I am going, O my people,
On a long and distant journey;
Many moons and many winters
Will have come, and will have vanished,
Ere I come again to see you.
But my guests I leave behind me;
Listen to their words of wisdom,
Listen to the truth they tell you,
For the Master of Life has sent them
From the land of light and morning!"

On the shore stood Hiawatha,
Turned and waved his hand at parting;
On the clear and luminous water
Launched his birch canoe for sailing,
From the pebbles of the margin
Shoved it forth into the water;
Whispered to it, "Westward! westward!"
And with speed it darted forward.

And the evening sun descending
Set the clouds on fire with redness,
Burned the broad sky, like a prairie,
Left upon the level water
One long track and trail of splendor,
Down whose stream, as down a river,
Westward, westward Hiawatha
Sailed into the fiery sunset,
Sailed into the purple vapors,
Sailed into the dusk of evening.

And the people from the margin
Watched him floating, rising, sinking,

Till the birch canoe seemed lifted
High into that sea of splendor,
Till it sank into the vapors
Like the new moon slowly, slowly
Sinking in the purple distance.

    And they said, "Farewell forever!"
Said, "Farewell, O Hiawatha!"
And the forests, dark and lonely,
Moved through all their depths of darkness,
Sighed, "Farewell, O Hiawatha!"
And the waves upon the margin
Rising, rippling on the pebbles,
Sobbed, "Farewell, O Hiawatha!"
And the heron, the Shuh-shuh-gah,
From her haunts among the fen-lands,
Screamed, "Farewell, O Hiawatha!"

    Thus departed Hiawatha,
Hiawatha the Beloved,
In the glory of the sunset,
In the purple mists of evening,
To the regions of the home-wind,
Of the Northwest-Wind, Keewaydin,
To the Islands of the Blessed,
To the Kingdom of Ponemah,
To the Land of the Hereafter!

My Lost Youth

Often I think of the beautiful town
    That is seated by the sea;
Often in thought go up and down
The pleasant streets of that dear old town,
    And my youth comes back to me.
      And a verse of a Lapland song
      Is haunting my memory still:
      "A boy's will is the wind's will,
And the thoughts of youth are long, long thoughts."

I can see the shadowy lines of its trees,
    And catch, in sudden gleams,
The sheen of the far-surrounding seas,
And islands that were the Hesperides
    Of all my boyish dreams.
      And the burden of that old song,
      It murmurs and whispers still:
      "A boy's will is the wind's will,
And the thoughts of youth are long, long thoughts."

I remember the black wharves and the slips,
    And the sea-tides tossing free;
And Spanish sailors with bearded lips,
And the beauty and mystery of the ships,
    And the magic of the sea.
      And the voice of that wayward song
      Is singing and saying still:
      "A boy's will is the wind's will,
And the thoughts of youth are long, long thoughts."
I remember the bulwarks by the shore,

And the fort upon the hill;
The sunrise gun, with its hollow roar,
The drum-beat repeated o'er and o'er,
And the bugle wild and shrill.
And the music of that old song
Throbs in my memory still:
"A boy's will is the wind's will,
And the thoughts of youth are long, long thoughts."

I remember the sea-fight far away,
How it thundered o'er the tide!
And the dead captains, as they lay
In their graves, o'erlooking the tranquil bay,
Where they in battle died.
And the sound of that mournful song
Goes through me with a thrill:
"A boy's will is the wind's will,
And the thoughts of youth are long, long thoughts."

I can see the breezy dome of groves,
The shadows of Deering's Woods;
And the friendships old and the early loves
Come back with a Sabbath sound, as of doves
In quiet neighborhoods.
And the verse of that sweet old song,
It flutters and murmurs still:
"A boy's will is the wind's will,
And the thoughts of youth are long, long thoughts."

I remember the gleams and glooms that dart
Across the school-boy's brain;
The song and the silence in the heart,

That in part are prophecies, and in part
        Are longings wild and vain.
            And the voice of that fitful song
            Sings on, and is never still:
            "A boy's will is the wind's will,
And the thoughts of youth are long, long thoughts."

There are things of which I may not speak;
        There are dreams that cannot die;
There are thoughts that make the strong heart weak,
And bring a pallor into the cheek,
        And a mist before the eye.
            And the words of that fatal song
            Come over me like a chill:
            "A boy's will is the wind's will,
And the thoughts of youth are long, long thoughts."

Strange to me now are the forms I meet
        When I visit the dear old town;
But the native air is pure and sweet,
And the trees that o'ershadow each well-known street,
        As they balance up and down,
            Are singing the beautiful song,
            Are sighing and whispering still:
            "A boy's will is the wind's will,
And the thoughts of youth are long, long thoughts."

And Deering's Woods are fresh and fair,
        And with joy that is almost pain
My heart goes back to wander there,
And among the dreams of the days that were,
        I find my lost youth again.

And the strange and beautiful song,
The groves are repeating it still:
"A boy's will is the wind's will,
And the thoughts of youth are long, long thoughts."

The Ladder of St Augustine

Saint Augustine! well hast thou said,
    That of our vices we can frame
A ladder, if we will but tread
    Beneath our feet each deed of shame!

All common things, each day's events,
    That with the hour begin and end,
Our pleasures and our discontents,
    Are rounds by which we may ascend.

The low desire, the base design,
    That makes another's virtues less;
The revel of the ruddy wine,
    And all occasions of excess;

The longing for ignoble things;
    The strife for triumph more than truth;
The hardening of the heart, that brings
    Irreverence for the dreams of youth;

All thoughts of ill; all evil deeds,
    That have their root in thoughts of ill;
Whatever hinders or impedes
    The action of the nobler will;—

All these must first be trampled down
    Beneath our feet, if we would gain
In the bright fields of fair renown
    The right of eminent domain.

We have not wings, we cannot soar;
    But we have feet to scale and climb
By slow degrees, by more and more,
    The cloudy summits of our time.

The mighty pyramids of stone
    That wedge-like cleave the desert airs,
When nearer seen, and better known,
    Are but gigantic flights of stairs.

The distant mountains, that uprear
    Their solid bastions to the skies,
Are crossed by pathways, that appear
    As we to higher levels rise.

The heights by great men reached and kept
    Were not attained by sudden flight,
But they, while their companions slept,
    Were toiling upward in the night.

Standing on what too long we bore
    With shoulders bent and downcast eyes,
We may discern—unseen before—
    A path to higher destinies.

Nor deem the irrevocable Past,
    As wholly wasted, wholly vain,
If, rising on its wrecks, at last
    To something nobler we attain.

Haunted Houses

All houses wherein men have lived and died
    Are haunted houses. Through the open doors
The harmless phantoms on their errands glide,
    With feet that make no sound upon the floors.

We meet them at the doorway, on the stair,
    Along the passages they come and go,
Impalpable impressions on the air,
    A sense of something moving to and fro.

There are more guests at table than the hosts
    Invited; the illuminated hall
Is thronged with quiet, inoffensive ghosts,
    As silent as the pictures on the wall.

The stranger at my fireside cannot see
    The forms I see, nor hear the sounds I hear;
He but perceives what is; while unto me
    All that has been is visible and clear.

We have no title-deeds to house or lands;
    Owners and occupants of earlier dates
From graves forgotten stretch their dusty hands,
    And hold in mortmain still their old estates.

The spirit-world around this world of sense
    Floats like an atmosphere, and everywhere
Wafts through these earthly mists and vapors dense
    A vital breath of more ethereal air.

Our little lives are kept in equipoise
    By opposite attractions and desires;
The struggle of the instinct that enjoys,
    And the more noble instinct that aspires.

These perturbations, this perpetual jar
    Of earthly wants and aspirations high,
Come from the influence of an unseen star,
    An undiscovered planet in our sky.

And as the moon from some dark gate of cloud
    Throws o'er the sea a floating bridge of light,
Across whose trembling planks our fancies crowd
    Into the realm of mystery and night,—

So from the world of spirits there descends
    A bridge of light, connecting it with this,
O'er whose unsteady floor, that sways and bends,
    Wander our thoughts above the dark abyss.

Christmas Bells

I heard the bells on Christmas Day
Their old, familiar carols play,
    And wild and sweet
    The words repeat
Of peace on earth, good-will to men!

And thought how, as the day had come,
The belfries of all Christendom
    Had rolled along
    The unbroken song
Of peace on earth, good-will to men!

Till ringing, singing on its way,
The world revolved from night to day,
    A voice, a chime,
    A chant sublime
Of peace on earth, good-will to men!

Then from each black, accursed mouth
The cannon thundered in the South,
    And with the sound
    The carols drowned
Of peace on earth, good-will to men!

It was as if an earthquake rent
The hearth-stones of a continent,
    And made forlorn
    The households born
Of peace on earth, good-will to men!

And in despair I bowed my head;
"There is no peace on earth," I said;
     "For hate is strong,
     And mocks the song
Of peace on earth, good-will to men!"

Then pealed the bells more loud and deep:
"God is not dead, nor doth He sleep;
     The Wrong shall fail,
     The Right prevail,
With peace on earth, good-will to men."

Divina Commedia

I

Oft have I seen at some cathedral door
    A laborer, pausing in the dust and heat,
    Lay down his burden, and with reverent feet
    Enter, and cross himself, and on the floor
Kneel to repeat his paternoster o'er;
    Far off the noises of the world retreat;
    The loud vociferations of the street
    Become an undistinguishable roar.
So, as I enter here from day to day,
    And leave my burden at this minster gate,
    Kneeling in prayer, and not ashamed to pray,
The tumult of the time disconsolate
    To inarticulate murmurs dies away,
    While the eternal ages watch and wait.

II

How strange the sculptures that adorn these towers!
    This crowd of statues, in whose folded sleeves
    Birds build their nests; while canopied with leaves
    Parvis and portal bloom like trellised bowers,
And the vast minster seems a cross of flowers!
    But fiends and dragons on the gargoyled eaves
    Watch the dead Christ between the living thieves,
    And, underneath, the traitor Judas lowers!
Ah! from what agonies of heart and brain,
    What exultations trampling on despair,
    What tenderness, what tears, what hate of wrong,
What passionate outcry of a soul in pain,
    Uprose this poem of the earth and air,
    This mediæval miracle of song!

III

I enter, and I see thee in the gloom
    Of the long aisles, O poet saturnine!
    And strive to make my steps keep pace with thine.
    The air is filled with some unknown perfume;
The congregation of the dead make room
    For thee to pass; the votive tapers shine;
    Like rooks that haunt Ravenna's groves of pine
    The hovering echoes fly from tomb to tomb.
From the confessionals I hear arise
    Rehearsals of forgotten tragedies,
    And lamentations from the crypts below;
And then a voice celestial that begins
    With the pathetic words, "Although your sins
    As scarlet be," and ends with "as the snow."

IV

With snow-white veil and garments as of flame,
    She stands before thee, who so long ago
    Filled thy young heart with passion and the woe
    From which thy song and all its splendors came;
And while with stern rebuke she speaks thy name,
    The ice about thy heart melts as the snow
    On mountain heights, and in swift overflow
    Comes gushing from thy lips in sobs of shame.
Thou makest full confession; and a gleam,
    As of the dawn on some dark forest cast,
    Seems on thy lifted forehead to increase;
Lethe and Eunoë—the remembered dream
    And the forgotten sorrow—bring at last
    That perfect pardon which is perfect peace.

V

I lift mine eyes, and all the windows blaze
    With forms of Saints and holy men who died,
    Here martyred and hereafter glorified;
    And the great Rose upon its leaves displays
Christ's Triumph, and the angelic roundelays,
    With splendor upon splendor multiplied;
    And Beatrice again at Dante's side
    No more rebukes, but smiles her words of praise.
And then the organ sounds, and unseen choirs
    Sing the old Latin hymns of peace and love
    And benedictions of the Holy Ghost;
And the melodious bells among the spires
    O'er all the house-tops and through heaven above
    Proclaim the elevation of the Host!

VI

O star of morning and of liberty!
    O bringer of the light, whose splendor shines
    Above the darkness of the Apennines,
    Forerunner of the day that is to be!
The voices of the city and the sea,
    The voices of the mountains and the pines,
    Repeat thy song, till the familiar lines
    Are footpaths for the thought of Italy!
Thy fame is blown abroad from all the heights,
    Through all the nations, and a sound is heard,
    As of a mighty wind, and men devout,
Strangers of Rome, and the new proselytes,
    In their own language hear thy wondrous word,
    And many are amazed and many doubt.

Giotto's Tower

How many lives, made beautiful and sweet
    By self-devotion and by self-restraint,
    Whose pleasure is to run without complaint
    On unknown errands of the Paraclete,
Wanting the reverence of unshodden feet,
    Fail of the nimbus which the artists paint
    Around the shining forehead of the saint,
    And are in their completeness incomplete!
In the old Tuscan town stands Giotto's tower,
    The lily of Florence blossoming in stone,—
    A vision, a delight, and a desire,—
The builder's perfect and centennial flower,
    That in the night of ages bloomed alone,
    But wanting still the glory of the spire.

The Two Angels

Two angels, one of Life and one of Death,
　　Passed o'er our village as the morning broke;
The dawn was on their faces, and beneath,
　　The sombre houses hearsed with plumes of smoke.

Their attitude and aspect were the same,
　　Alike their features and their robes of white;
But one was crowned with amaranth, as with flame,
　　And one with asphodels, like flakes of light.

I saw them pause on their celestial way;
　　Then said I, with deep fear and doubt oppressed,
"Beat not so loud, my heart, lest thou betray
　　The place where thy beloved are at rest!"

And he who wore the crown of asphodels,
　　Descending, at my door began to knock,
And my soul sank within me, as in wells
　　The waters sink before an earthquake's shock.

I recognized the nameless agony,
　　The terror and the tremor and the pain,
That oft before had filled or haunted me,
　　And now returned with threefold strength again.

The door I opened to my heavenly guest,
　　And listened, for I thought I heard God's voice;
And, knowing whatsoe'er he sent was best,
　　Dared neither to lament nor to rejoice.

Then with a smile, that filled the house with light,
        "My errand is not Death, but Life," he said;
And ere I answered, passing out of sight,
        On his celestial embassy he sped.

'Twas at thy door, O friend! and not at mine,
        The angel with the amaranthine wreath,
Pausing, descended, and with voice divine,
        Whispered a word that had a sound like Death.

Then fell upon the house a sudden gloom,
        A shadow on those features fair and thin;
And softly, from that hushed and darkened room,
        Two angels issued, where but one went in.

All is of God! If he but wave his hand,
        The mists collect, the rain falls thick and loud,
Till, with a smile of light on sea and land,
        Lo! he looks back from the departing cloud.

Angels of Life and Death alike are his;
        Without his leave they pass no threshold o'er;
Who, then, would wish or dare, believing this,
        Against his messengers to shut the door?

The Children's Hour

Between the dark and the daylight,
        When the night is beginning to lower,
Comes a pause in the day's occupations,
        That is known as the Children's Hour.

I hear in the chamber above me
        The patter of little feet,
The sound of a door that is opened,
        And voices soft and sweet.

From my study I see in the lamplight,
        Descending the broad hall stair,
Grave Alice, and laughing Allegra,
        And Edith with golden hair.

A whisper, and then a silence:
        Yet I know by their merry eyes
They are plotting and planning together
        To take me by surprise.

A sudden rush from the stairway,
        A sudden raid from the hall!
By three doors left unguarded
        They enter my castle wall!

They climb up into my turret
        O'er the arms and back of my chair;
If I try to escape, they surround me;
        They seem to be everywhere.

They almost devour me with kisses,
    Their arms about me entwine,
Till I think of the Bishop of Bingen
    In his Mouse-Tower on the Rhine!

Do you think, O blue-eyed banditti,
    Because you have scaled the wall,
Such an old mustache as I am
    Is not a match for you all!

I have you fast in my fortress,
    And will not let you depart,
But put you down into the dungeon
    In the round-tower of my heart.

And there will I keep you forever,
    Yes, forever and a day,
Till the walls shall crumble to ruin,
    And moulder in dust away!

The Theologian's Tale

In the heroic days when Ferdinand
And Isabella ruled the Spanish land,
And Torquemada, with his subtle brain,
Ruled them, as Grand Inquisitor of Spain,
In a great castle near Valladolid,
Moated and high and by fair woodlands hid,
There dwelt as from the chronicles we learn,
An old Hidalgo proud and taciturn,
Whose name has perished, with his towers of stone,
And all his actions save this one alone;
This one, so terrible, perhaps 'twere best
If it, too, were forgotten with the rest;
Unless, perchance, our eyes can see therein
The martyrdom triumphant o'er the sin;
A double picture, with its gloom and glow,
The splendor overhead, the death below.

This sombre man counted each day as lost
On which his feet no sacred threshold crossed;
And when he chanced the passing Host to meet,
He knelt and prayed devoutly in the street;
Oft he confessed; and with each mutinous thought,
As with wild beasts at Ephesus, he fought.
In deep contrition scourged himself in Lent,
Walked in processions, with his head down bent,
At plays of Corpus Christi oft was seen,
And on Palm Sunday bore his bough of green.
His sole diversion was to hunt the boar
Through tangled thickets of the forest hoar,
Or with his jingling mules to hurry down

To some grand bull-fight in the neighboring town,
Or in the crowd with lighted taper stand,
When Jews were burned, or banished from the land.
Then stirred within him a tumultuous joy;
The demon whose delight is to destroy
Shook him, and shouted with a trumpet tone,
"Kill! kill! and let the Lord find out his own!"

And now, in that old castle in the wood,
His daughters, in the dawn of womanhood,
Returning from their convent school, had made
Resplendent with their bloom the forest shade,
Reminding him of their dead mother's face,
When first she came into that gloomy place,—
A memory in his heart as dim and sweet
As moonlight in a solitary street,
Where the same rays, that lift the sea, are thrown
Lovely but powerless upon walls of stone.
These two fair daughters of a mother dead
Were all the dream had left him as it fled.
A joy at first, and then a growing care,
As if a voice within him cried, "Beware!"
A vague presentiment of impending doom,
Like ghostly footsteps in a vacant room,
Haunted him day and night; a formless fear
That death to some one of his house was near,
With dark surmises of a hidden crime,
Made life itself a death before its time.
Jealous, suspicious, with no sense of shame,
A spy upon his daughters he became;
With velvet slippers, noiseless on the floors,
He glided softly through half-open doors;

Now in the room, and now upon the stair,
He stood beside them ere they were aware;
He listened in the passage when they talked,
He watched them from the casement when they walked,
He saw the gypsy haunt the river's side,
He saw the monk among the cork-trees glide;
And, tortured by the mystery and the doubt
Of some dark secret, past his finding out,
Baffled he paused; then reassured again
Pursued the flying phantom of his brain.
He watched them even when they knelt in church;
And then, descending lower in his search,
Questioned the servants, and with eager eyes
Listened incredulous to their replies;
The gypsy? none had seen her in the wood!
The monk? a mendicant in search of food!

At length the awful revelation came,
Crushing at once his pride of birth and name;
The hopes his yearning bosom forward cast,
And the ancestral glories of the vast,
All fell together, crumbling in disgrace,
A turret rent from battlement to base.
His daughters talking in the dead of night
In their own chamber, and without a light,
Listening, as he was wont, he overheard,
And learned the dreadful secret, word by word;
And hurrying from his castle, with a cry
He raised his hands to the unpitying sky,
Repeating one dread word, till bush and tree
Caught it, and shuddering answered, "Heresy!"
Wrapped in his cloak, his hat drawn o'er his face,

Now hurrying forward, now with lingering pace,
He walked all night the alleys of his park,
With one unseen companion in the dark,
The Demon who within him lay in wait,
And by his presence turned his love to hate,
Forever muttering in an undertone,
"Kill! kill! and let the Lord find out his own!"

Upon the morrow, after early Mass,
While yet the dew was glistening on the grass,
And all the woods were musical with birds,
The old Hidalgo, uttering fearful words,
Walked homeward with the Priest, and in his room
Summoned his trembling daughters to their doom.
When questioned, with brief answers they replied,
Nor when accused evaded or denied;
Expostulations, passionate appeals,
All that the human heart most fears or feels,
In vain the Priest with earnest voice essayed;
In vain the father threatened, wept, and prayed;
Until at last he said, with haughty mien,
"The Holy Office, then, must intervene!"

And now the Grand Inquisitor of Spain,
With all the fifty horsemen of his train,
His awful name resounding, like the blast
Of funeral trumpets, as he onward passed,
Came to Valladolid, and there began
To harry the rich Jews with fire and ban.
To him the Hidalgo went, and at the gate
Demanded audience on affairs of state,

And in a secret chamber stood before
A venerable graybeard of fourscore,
Dressed in the hood and habit of a friar;
Out of his eyes flashed a consuming fire,
And in his hand the mystic horn he held,
Which poison and all noxious charms dispelled.
He heard in silence the Hidalgo's tale,
Then answered in a voice that made him quail:
"Son of the Church! when Abraham of old
To sacrifice his only son was told,
He did not pause to parley nor protest
But hastened to obey the Lord's behest.
In him it was accounted righteousness;
The Holy Church expects of thee no less!"

A sacred frenzy seized the father's brain,
And Mercy from that hour implored in vain.
Ah! who will e'er believe the words I say?
His daughters he accused, and the same day
They both were cast into the dungeon's gloom,
That dismal antechamber of the tomb,
Arraigned, condemned, and sentenced to the flame,
The secret torture and the public shame.

Then to the Grand Inquisitor once more
The Hidalgo went, more eager than before,
And said: "When Abraham offered up his son,
He clave the wood wherewith it might be done.
By his example taught, let me too bring
Wood from the forest for my offering!"
And the deep voice, without a pause, replied:

"Son of the Church! by faith now justified,
Complete thy sacrifice, even as thou wilt;
The Church absolves thy conscience from all guilt!"

Then this most wretched father went his way
Into the woods, that round his castle lay,
Where once his daughters in their childhood played
With their young mother in the sun and shade.
Now all the leaves had fallen; the branches bare
Made a perpetual moaning in the air,
And screaming from their eyries overhead
The ravens sailed athwart the sky of lead.
With his own hands he lopped the boughs and bound
Fagots, that crackled with foreboding sound,
And on his mules, caparisoned and gay
With bells and tassels, sent them on their way.

Then with his mind on one dark purpose bent,
Again to the Inquisitor he went,
And said: "Behold, the fagots I have brought,
And now, lest my atonement be as naught,
Grant me one more request, one last desire,—
With my own hand to light the funeral fire!"
And Torquemada answered from his seat,
"Son of the Church! Thine offering is complete;
Her servants through all ages shall not cease
To magnify thy deed. Depart in peace!"

Upon the market-place, builded of stone
The scaffold rose, whereon Death claimed his own.
At the four corners, in stern attitude,
Four statues of the Hebrew Prophets stood,

Gazing with calm indifference in their eyes
Upon this place of human sacrifice,
Round which was gathering fast the eager crowd,
With clamor of voices dissonant and loud,
And every roof and window was alive
With restless gazers, swarming like a hive.

The church-bells tolled, the chant of monks drew near,
Loud trumpets stammered forth their notes of fear,
A line of torches smoked along the street,
There was a stir, a rush, a tramp of feet,
And, with its banners floating in the air,
Slowly the long procession crossed the square,
And, to the statues of the Prophets bound,
The victims stood, with fagots piled around.
Then all the air a blast of trumpets shook,
And louder sang the monks with bell and book,
And the Hidalgo, lofty, stern, and proud,
Lifted his torch, and, bursting through the crowd,
Lighted in haste the fagots, and then fled,
Lest those imploring eyes should strike him dead!

O pitiless skies! why did your clouds retain
For peasants' fields their floods of hoarded rain?
O pitiless earth! why open no abyss
To bury in its chasm a crime like this?

That night a mingled column of fire and smoke
From the dark thickets of the forest broke,
And, glaring o'er the landscape leagues away,
Made all the fields and hamlets bright as day.
Wrapped in a sheet of flame the castle blazed,

And as the villagers in terror gazed,
They saw the figure of that cruel knight
Lean from a window in the turret's height,
His ghastly face illumined with the glare,
His hands upraised above his head in prayer,
Till the floor sank beneath him, and he fell
Down the black hollow of that burning well.

Three centuries and more above his bones
Have piled the oblivious years like funeral stones;
His name has perished with him, and no trace
Remains on earth of his afflicted race;
But Torquemada's name, with clouds o'ercast,
Looms in the distant landscape of the Past,
Like a burnt tower upon a blackened heath,
Lit by the fires of burning woods beneath!

The Saga of King Olaf

The Challenge of Thor

I am the God Thor,
I am the War God,
I am the Thunderer!
Here in my Northland,
My fastness and fortress,
Reign I forever!

Here amid icebergs
Rule I the nations;
This is my hammer,
Miölner the mighty;
Giants and sorcerers
Cannot withstand it!

These are the gauntlets
Wherewith I wield it,
And hurl it afar off;
This is my girdle;
Whenever I brace it,
Strength is redoubled!

The light thou beholdest
Stream through the heavens,
In flashes of crimson,
Is but my red beard
Blown by the night-wind,
Affrighting the nations!

Jove is my brother;
Mine eyes are the lightning;
The wheels of my chariot
Roll in the thunder,
The blows of my hammer
Ring in the earthquake!

Force rules the world still,
Has ruled it, shall rule it;
Meekness is weakness,
Strength is triumphant,
Over the whole earth
Still is it Thor's-Day!

Thou art a God too,
O Galilean!
And thus single-handed
Unto the combat,
Gauntlet or Gospel,
Here I defy thee!

King Olaf's Return

And King Olaf heard the cry,
Saw the red light in the sky,
  Laid his hand upon his sword,
As he leaned upon the railing,
And his ships went sailing, sailing
  Northward into Drontheim fiord.

There he stood as one who dreamed;
And the red light glanced and gleamed
  On the armor that he wore;

And he shouted, as the rifted
Streamers o'er him shook and shifted,
    "I accept thy challenge, Thor!"

To avenge his father slain,
And reconquer realm and reign,
    Came the youthful Olaf home,
Through the midnight sailing, sailing,
Listening to the wild wind's wailing,
    And the dashing of the foam.

To his thoughts the sacred name
Of his mother Astrid came,
    And the tale she oft had told
Of her flight by secret passes
Through the mountains and morasses,
    To the home of Hakon old.

Then strange memories crowded back
Of Queen Gunhild's wrath and wrack,
    And a hurried flight by sea;
Of grim Vikings, and the rapture
Of the sea-fight, and the capture,
    And the life of slavery.

How a stranger watched his face
In the Esthonian market-place,
    Scanned his features one by one,
Saying, "We should know each other;
I am Sigurd, Astrid's brother,
    Thou art Olaf, Astrid's son!"

Then as Queen Allogia's page,
Old in honors, young in age,
  Chief of all her men-at-arms;
Till vague whispers, and mysterious,
Reached King Valdemar, the imperious,
  Filling him with strange alarms.

Then his cruisings o'er the seas,
Westward to the Hebrides,
  And to Scilly's rocky shore;
And the hermit's cavern dismal,
Christ's great name and rites baptismal
  In the ocean's rush and roar.

All these thoughts of love and strife
Glimmered through his lurid life,
  As the stars' intenser light
Through the red flames o'er him trailing,
As his ships went sailing, sailing,
  Northward in the summer night.

Trained for either camp or court,
Skilful in each manly sport,
  Young and beautiful and tall;
Art of warfare, craft of chases,
Swimming, skating, snow-shoe races
  Excellent alike in all.

When at sea, with all his rowers,
He along the bending oars
  Outside of his ship could run.
He the Smalsor Horn ascended,

And his shining shield suspended,
    On its summit, like a sun.

On the ship-rails he could stand,
Wield his sword with either hand,
    And at once two javelins throw;
At all feasts where ale was strongest
Sat the merry monarch longest,
    First to come and last to go.

Norway never yet had seen
One so beautiful of mien,
    One so royal in attire,
When in arms completely furnished,
Harness gold-inlaid and burnished,
    Mantle like a flame of fire.

Thus came Olaf to his own,
When upon the night-wind blown
    Passed that cry along the shore;
And he answered, while the rifted
Streamers o'er him shook and shifted,
    "I accept thy challenge, Thor!"

Thora of Rimol

"Thora of Rimol! hide me! hide me!
Danger and shame and death betide me!
For Olaf the King is hunting me down
Through field and forest, through thorp and town!"
        Thus cried Jarl Hakon
        To Thora, the fairest of women.

Hakon Jarl! for the love I bear thee
Neither shall shame nor death come near thee!
But the hiding-place wherein thou must lie
Is the cave underneath the swine in the sty.
  "Thus to Jarl Hakon"
  Said Thora, the fairest of women.

So Hakon Jarl and his base thrall Karker
Crouched in the cave, than a dungeon darker,
As Olaf came riding, with men in mail,
Through the forest roads into Orkadale,
  Demanding Jarl Hakon
  Of Thora, the fairest of women.

"Rich and honored shall be whoever
The head of Hakon Jarl shall dissever!"
Hakon heard him, and Karker the slave,
Through the breathing-holes of the darksome cave.
  Alone in her chamber
  Wept Thora, the fairest of women.

Said Karker, the crafty, "I will not slay thee!
For all the king's gold I will never betray thee!"
"Then why dost thou turn so pale, O churl,
And then again black as the earth?" said the Earl.
  More pale and more faithful
  Was Thora, the fairest of women.

From a dream in the night the thrall started, saying,
"Round my neck a gold ring King Olaf was laying!"
And Hakon answered, "Beware of the king!
He will lay round thy neck a blood-red ring."

At the ring on her finger
Gazed Thora, the fairest of women.

At daybreak slept Hakon, with sorrows encumbered,
But screamed and drew up his feet as he slumbered;
The thrall in the darkness plunged with his knife,
And the Earl awakened no more in this life.
　　But wakeful and weeping
　　Sat Thora, the fairest of women.

At Nidarholm the priests are all singing,
Two ghastly heads on the gibbet are swinging;
One is Jarl Hakon's and one is his thrall's,
And the people are shouting from windows and walls;
　　While alone in her chamber
　　Swoons Thora, the fairest of women.

Queen Sigrid the Haughty

Queen Sigrid the Haughty sat proud and aloft
In her chamber, that looked over meadow and croft.
　　Heart's dearest,
　　Why dost thou sorrow so?

The floor with tassels of fir was besprent,
Filling the room with their fragrant scent.

She heard the birds sing, she saw the sun shine,
The air of summer was sweeter than wine.

Like a sword without scabbard the bright river lay
Between her own kingdom and Norroway.

But Olaf the King had sued for her hand,
The sword would be sheathed, the river be spanned.

Her maidens were seated around her knee,
Working bright figures in tapestry.

And one was singing the ancient rune
Of Brynhilda's love and the wrath of Gudrun.

And through it, and round it, and over it all
Sounded incessant the waterfall.

The Queen in her hand held a ring of gold,
From the door of Ladé's Temple old.

King Olaf had sent her this wedding gift,
But her thoughts as arrows were keen and swift.

She had given the ring to her goldsmiths twain,
Who smiled, as they handed it back again.

And Sigrid the Queen, in her haughty way,
Said, "Why do you smile, my goldsmiths, say?"

And they answered: "O Queen! if the truth must be told,
The ring is of copper, and not of gold!"

The lightning flashed o'er her forehead and cheek,
She only murmured, she did not speak:

"If in his gifts he can faithless be,
There will be no gold in his love to me."

A footstep was heard on the outer stair,
And in strode King Olaf with royal air.

He kissed the Queen's hand, and he whispered of love,
And swore to be true as the stars are above.

But she smiled with contempt as she answered: "O King,
Will you swear it, as Odin once swore, on the ring?"

And the King: "O speak not of Odin to me,
The wife of King Olaf a Christian must be."

Looking straight at the King, with her level brows,
She said, "I keep true to my faith and my vows."

Then the face of King Olaf was darkened with gloom,
He rose in his anger and strode through the room.

"Why, then, should I care to have thee?" he said,—
"A faded old woman, a heathenish jade!"

His zeal was stronger than fear or love,
And he struck the Queen in the face with his glove.

Then forth from the chamber in anger he fled,
And the wooden stairway shook with his tread.
Queen Sigrid the Haughty said under her breath,
"This insult, King Olaf, shall be thy death!"
  Heart's dearest,
  Why dost thou sorrow so?

The Skerry of Shrieks

Now from all King Olaf's farms
       His men-at-arms
Gathered on the Eve of Easter;
To his house at Angvalds-ness
       Fast they press,
Drinking with the royal feaster.

Loudly through the wide-flung door
       Came the roar
Of the sea upon the Skerry;
And its thunder loud and near
       Reached the ear,
Mingling with their voices merry.

"Hark!" said Olaf to his Scald,
       Halfred the Bald,
"Listen to that song, and learn it!
Half my kingdom would I give,
       As I live,
If by such songs you would earn it!"

"For of all the runes and rhymes
       Of all times,
Best I like the ocean's dirges,
When the old harper heaves and rocks,
       His hoary locks
Flowing and flashing in the surges!"

Halfred answered: "I am called
       The Unappalled!

Nothing hinders me or daunts me.
Hearken to me, then, O King,
  While I sing
The great Ocean Song that haunts me."

"I will hear your song sublime
  Some other time,"
Says the drowsy monarch, yawning,
And retires; each laughing guest
  Applauds the jest;
Then they sleep till day is dawning.

Facing up and down the yard,
  King Olaf's guard
Saw the sea-mist slowly creeping
O'er the sands, and up the hill,
  Gathering still
Round the house where they were sleeping.

It was not the fog he saw,
  Nor misty flaw,
That above the landscape brooded;
It was Eyvind Kallda's crew
  Of warlocks blue
With their caps of darkness hooded!

Round and round the house they go,
  Weaving slow
Magic circles to encumber
And imprison in their ring
  Olaf the King,
As he helpless lies in slumber.

Then athwart the vapors dun
      The Easter sun
Streamed with one broad track of splendor!
In their real forms appeared
      The warlocks weird,
Awful as the Witch of Endor.

Blinded by the light that glared,
      They groped and stared
Round about with steps unsteady;
From his window Olaf gazed,
      And, amazed,
"Who are these strange people?" said he.

"Eyvind Kallda and his men!"
      Answered then
From the yard a sturdy farmer;
While the men-at-arms apace
      Filled the place,
Busily buckling on their armor.

From the gates they sallied forth,
      South and north,
Scoured the island coast around them,
Seizing all the warlock band,
      Foot and hand
On the Skerry's rocks they bound them.

And at eve the king again
      Called his train,
And, with all the candles burning,
Silent sat and heard once more

The sullen roar
Of the ocean tides returning.

Shrieks and cries of wild despair
      Filled the air,
Growing fainter as they listened;
Then the bursting surge alone
      Sounded on;—
Thus the sorcerers were christened!

"Sing, O Scald, your song sublime,
      Your ocean-rhyme,"
Cried King Olaf: "it will cheer me!"
Said the Scald, with pallid cheeks,
      "The Skerry of Shrieks
Sings too loud for you to hear me!"

The Wraith of Odin

The guests were loud, the ale was strong,
King Olaf feasted late and long;
The hoary Scalds together sang;
O'erhead the smoky rafters rang.
      Dead rides Sir Morten of Fogelsang.

The door swung wide, with creak and din;
A blast of cold night-air came in,
And on the threshold shivering stood
A one-eyed guest, with cloak and hood.
      Dead rides Sir Morten of Fogelsang.

The King exclaimed, "O graybeard pale!
Come warm thee with this cup of ale."

The foaming draught the old man quaffed,
The noisy guests looked on and laughed.
    Dead rides Sir Morten of Fogelsang.

Then spake the King: "Be not afraid;
Sit here by me." The guest obeyed,
And, seated at the table, told
Tales of the sea, and Sagas old.
    Dead rides Sir Morten of Fogelsang.

And ever, when the tale was o'er,
The King demanded yet one more;
Till Sigurd the Bishop smiling said,
"'Tis late, O King, and time for bed."
    Dead rides Sir Morten of Fogelsang.

The King retired; the stranger guest
Followed and entered with the rest;
The lights were out, the pages gone,
But still the garrulous guest spake on.
    Dead rides Sir Morten of Fogelsang.

As one who from a volume reads,
He spake of heroes and their deeds,
Of lands and cities he had seen,
And stormy gulfs that tossed between.
    Dead rides Sir Morten of Fogelsang.

Then from his lips in music rolled
The Havamal of Odin old,
With sounds mysterious as the roar

Of billows on a distant shore.
     Dead rides Sir Morten of Fogelsang.

"Do we not learn from runes and rhymes
Made by the gods in elder times,
And do not still the great Scalds teach
That silence better is than speech?"
     Dead rides Sir Morten of Fogelsang.

Smiling at this, the King replied,
"Thy lore is by thy tongue belied;
For never was I so enthralled
Either by Saga-man or Scald,"
     Dead rides Sir Morten of Fogelsang.

The Bishop said, "Late hours we keep!
Night wanes, O King! 'tis time for sleep!"
Then slept the King, and when he woke
The guest was gone, the morning broke.
     Dead rides Sir Morten of Fogelsang.

They found the doors securely barred,
They found the watch-dog in the yard,
There was no footprint in the grass,
And none had seen the stranger pass.
     Dead rides Sir Morten of Fogelsang.

King Olaf crossed himself and said:
"I know that Odin the Great is dead;
Sure is the triumph of our Faith,
The one-eyed stranger was his wraith."
     Dead rides Sir Morten of Fogelsang.

Iron-Beard

Olaf the King, one summer morn,
Blew a blast on his bugle-horn,
Sending his signal through the land of Drontheim.

And to the Hus-Ting held at Mere
Gathered the farmers far and near,
With their war weapons ready to confront him.

Ploughing under the morning star,
Old Iron-Beard in Yriar
Heard the summons, chuckling with a low laugh.

He wiped the sweat-drops from his brow,
Unharnessed his horses from the plough,
And clattering came on horseback to King Olaf.

He was the churliest of the churls;
Little he cared for king or earls;
Bitter as home-brewed ale were his foaming passions.

Hodden-gray was the garb he wore,
And by the Hammer of Thor he swore;
He hated the narrow town, and all its fashions.

But he loved the freedom of his farm,
His ale at night, by the fireside warm,
Gudrun his daughter, with her flaxen tresses.

He loved his horses and his herds,
The smell of the earth, and the song of birds,
His well-filled barns, his brook with its water-cresses.

Huge and cumbersome was his frame;
His beard, from which he took his name,
Frosty and fierce, like that of Hymer the Giant.

So at the Hus-Ting he appeared,
The farmer of Yriar, Iron-Beard,
On horseback, in an attitude defiant.

And to King Olaf he cried aloud,
Out of the middle of the crowd,
That tossed about him like a stormy ocean:

"Such sacrifices shalt thou bring;
To Odin and to Thor, O King,
As other kings have done in their devotion!"

King Olaf answered: "I command
This land to be a Christian land;
Here is my Bishop who the folk baptizes!"

"But if you ask me to restore
Your sacrifices, stained with gore,
Then will I offer human sacrifices!"

"Not slaves and peasants shall they be,
But men of note and high degree,
Such men as Orm of Lyra and Kar of Gryting!"

Then to their Temple strode he in,
And loud behind him heard the din
Of his men-at-arms and the peasants fiercely fighting.

There in the Temple, carved in wood,
The image of great Odin stood,
And other gods, with Thor supreme among them.

King Olaf smote them with the blade
Of his huge war-axe, gold inlaid,
And downward shattered to the pavement flung them.

At the same moment rose without,
From the contending crowd, a shout,
A mingled sound of triumph and of wailing.

And there upon the trampled plain
The farmer Iron-Beard lay slain,
Midway between the assailed and the assailing.

King Olaf from the doorway spoke.
"Choose ye between two things, my folk,
To be baptized or given up to slaughter!"

And seeing their leader stark and dead,
The people with a murmur said,
"O King, baptize us with thy holy water";

So all the Drontheim land became
A Christian land in name and fame,
In the old gods no more believing and trusting.

And as a blood-atonement, soon
King Olaf wed the fair Gudrun;
And thus in peace ended the Drontheim Hus-Ting!

Gudrun

On King Olaf's bridal night
Shines the moon with tender light,
And across the chamber streams
Its tide of dreams.

At the fatal midnight hour,
When all evil things have power,
In the glimmer of the moon
Stands Gudrun.

Close against her heaving breast
Something in her hand is pressed
Like an icicle, its sheen
Is cold and keen.

On the cairn are fixed her eyes
Where her murdered father lies,
And a voice remote and drear
She seems to hear.

What a bridal night is this!
Cold will be the dagger's kiss;
Laden with the chill of death
Is its breath.

Like the drifting snow she sweeps
To the couch where Olaf sleeps;
Suddenly he wakes and stirs,
　　His eyes meet hers.

"What is that," King Olaf said,
"Gleams so bright above thy head?
Wherefore standest thou so white
　　In pale moonlight?"

"'Tis the bodkin that I wear
When at night I bind my hair;
It woke me falling on the floor;
　　'Tis nothing more."

"Forests have ears, and fields have eyes;
Often treachery lurking lies
Underneath the fairest hair!
　　Gudrun beware!"

Ere the earliest peep of morn
Blew King Olaf's bugle-horn;
And forever sundered ride
　　Bridegroom and bride!

Thangbrand the Priest

Short of stature, large of limb,
　　Burly face and russet beard,
All the women stared at him,
　　When in Iceland he appeared.

  "Look!" they said,
  With nodding head,
"There goes Thangbrand, Olaf's Priest."

All the prayers he knew by rote,
 He could preach like Chrysostome,
From the Fathers he could quote,
 He had even been at Rome,
  A learned clerk,
  A man of mark,
Was this Thangbrand, Olaf's Priest,

He was quarrelsome and loud,
 And impatient of control,
Boisterous in the market crowd,
 Boisterous at the wassail-bowl,
  Everywhere
  Would drink and swear,
Swaggering Thangbrand, Olaf's Priest

In his house this malcontent
 Could the King no longer bear,
So to Iceland he was sent
 To convert the heathen there,
  And away
  One summer day
Sailed this Thangbrand, Olaf's Priest.

There in Iceland, o'er their books
 Pored the people day and night,
But he did not like their looks,
 Nor the songs they used to write.

                    "All this rhyme
                 Is waste of time!"
Grumbled Thangbrand, Olaf's Priest.

To the alehouse, where he sat
    Came the Scalds and Saga-men;
Is it to be wondered at,
    That they quarrelled now and then,
                When o'er his beer
                Began to leer
Drunken Thangbrand, Olaf's Priest?

All the folk in Altafiord
    Boasted of their island grand;
Saying in a single word,
    "Iceland is the finest land
                That the sun
                Doth shine upon!"
Loud laughed Thangbrand, Olaf's Priest.

And he answered: "What's the use
    Of this bragging up and down,
When three women and one goose
    Make a market in your town!"
                Every Scald
                Satires scrawled
On poor Thangbrand, Olaf's Priest.

Something worse they did than that;
    And what vexed him most of all
Was a figure in shovel hat,
    Drawn in charcoal on the wall;

With words that go
Sprawling below,
"This is Thangbrand, Olaf's Priest."

Hardly knowing what he did,
   Then he smote them might and main,
Thorvald Veile and Veterlid
   Lay there in the alehouse slain.
      "To-day we are gold,
      To-morrow mould!"
Muttered Thangbrand, Olaf's Priest.

Much in fear of axe and rope,
   Back to Norway sailed he then.
"O, King Olaf! little hope
   Is there of these Iceland men!"
      Meekly said,
      With bending head,
Pious Thangbrand, Olaf's Priest.

Raud the Strong

"All the old gods are dead,
All the wild warlocks fled;
But the White Christ lives and reigns,
And throughout my wide domains
His Gospel shall be spread!"
      On the Evangelists
      Thus swore King Olaf.

But still in dreams of the night
Beheld he the crimson light,
And heard the voice that defied

Him who was crucified,
And challenged him to the fight.
>   To Sigurd the Bishop
>   King Olaf confessed it.

And Sigurd the Bishop said,
"The old gods are not dead,
For the great Thor still reigns,
And among the Jarls and Thanes
The old witchcraft still is spread."
>   Thus to King Olaf
>   Said Sigurd the Bishop.

"Far north in the Salten Fiord,
By rapine, fire, and sword,
Lives the Viking, Raud the Strong;
All the Godoe Isles belong
To him and his heathen horde."
>   Thus went on speaking
>   Sigurd the Bishop.

"A warlock, a wizard is he,
And lord of the wind and the sea;
And whichever way he sails,
He has ever favoring gales,
By his craft in sorcery."
>   Here the sign of the cross
>   Made devoutly King Olaf.

"With rites that we both abhor,
He worships Odin and Thor;
So it cannot yet be said,

That all the old gods are dead,
And the warlocks are no more,"
    Flushing with anger
    Said Sigurd the Bishop.

Then King Olaf cried aloud:
"I will talk with this mighty Raud,
And along the Salten Fiord
Preach the Gospel with my sword,
Or be brought back in my shroud!"
    So northward from Drontheim
    Sailed King Olaf!

Bishop Sigurd at Salten Fiord

Loud the anngy wind was wailing
As King Olaf's ships came sailing
Northward out of Drontheim haven
    To the mouth of Salten Fiord.

Though the flying sea-spray drenches
Fore and aft the rowers' benches,
Not a single heart is craven
    Of the champions there on board.

All without the Fiord was quiet
But within it storm and riot,
Such as on his Viking cruises
    Raud the Strong was wont to ride.

And the sea through all its tide-ways
Swept the reeling vessels sideways,

As the leaves are swept through sluices,
    When the flood-gates open wide.

"'Tis the warlock! 'Tis the demon
Raud!" cried Sigurd to the seamen;
"But the Lord is not affrighted
    By the witchcraft of his foes."

To the ship's bow he ascended,
By his choristers attended,
Round him were the tapers lighted,
    And the sacred incense rose.

On the bow stood Bishop Sigurd,
In his robes, as one transfigured,
And the Crucifix he planted
    High amid the rain and mist.

Then with holy water sprinkled
All the ship; the mass-bells tinkled;
Loud the monks around him chanted,
    Loud he read the Evangelist.

As into the Fiord they darted,
On each side the water parted;
Down a path like silver molten
    Steadily rowed King Olaf's ships;

Steadily burned all night the tapers,
And the White Christ through the vapors
Gleamed across the Fiord of Salten,
    As through John's Apocalypse,—

Till at last they reached Raud's dwelling
On the little isle of Gelling;
Not a guard was at the doorway,
    Not a glimmer of light was seen.

But at anchor, carved and gilded,
Lay the dragon-ship he builded;
'Twas the grandest ship in Norway,
    With its crest and scales of green.

Up the stairway, softly creeping,
To the loft where Raud was sleeping,
With their fists they burst asunder
    Bolt and bar that held the door.

Drunken with sleep and ale they found him,
Dragged him from his bed and bound him,
While he stared with stupid wonder,
    At the look and garb they wore.

Then King Olaf said: "O Sea-King!
Little time have we for speaking,
Choose between the good and evil;
    Be baptized! or thou shalt die!"

But in scorn the heathen scoffer
Answered: "I disdain thine offer;
Neither fear I God nor Devil;
    Thee and thy Gospel I defy!"

Then between his jaws distended,
When his frantic struggles ended,

Through King Olaf's horn an adder,
      Touched by fire, they forced to glide.

Sharp his tooth was as an arrow,
As he gnawed through bone and marrow;
But without a groan or shudder,
      Raud the Strong blaspheming died.

Then baptized they all that region,
Swarthy Lap and fair Norwegian,
Far as swims the salmon, leaping,
      Up the streams of Salten Fiord.

In their temples Thor and Odin
Lay in dust and ashes trodden,
As King Olaf, onward sweeping,
      Preached the Gospel with his sword.

Then he took the carved and gilded
Dragon-ship that Raud had builded,
And the tiller single-handed,
      Grasping, steered into the main.

Southward sailed the sea-gulls o'er him,
Southward sailed the ship that bore him,
Till at Drontheim haven landed
      Olaf and his crew again.

King Olaf's Christmas

At Drontheim, Olaf the King
Heard the bells of Yule-tide ring,
      As he sat in his banquet-hall,

Drinking the nut-brown ale,
With his bearded Berserks hale
    And tall.

Three days his Yule-tide feasts
He held with Bishops and Priests,
    And his horn filled up to the brim;
But the ale was never too strong,
Nor the Saga-man's tale too long,
    For him.

O'er his drinking-horn, the sign
He made of the cross divine,
    As he drank, and muttered his prayers;
But the Berserks evermore
Made the sign of the Hammer of Thor
    Over theirs.

The gleams of the fire-light dance
Upon helmet and hauberk and lance,
    And laugh in the eyes of the King;
And he cries to Halfred the Scald,
Gray-bearded, wrinkled, and bald,
    "Sing!"

"Sing me a song divine,
With a sword in every line,
    And this shall be thy reward."
And he loosened the belt at his waist,
And in front of the singer placed
    His sword.

"Quern-biter of Hakon the Good,
Wherewith at a stroke he hewed
    The millstone through and through,
And Foot-breadth of Thoralf the Strong,
Were neither so broad nor so long,
    Nor so true."

Then the Scald took his harp and sang,
And loud though the music rang
    The sound of that shining word;
And the harp-strings a clangor made,
As if they were struck with the blade
    Of a sword.

And the Berserks round about
Broke forth into a shout
    That made the rafters ring:
They smote with their fists on the board,
And shouted, "Long live the Sword,
    And the King!"

But the King said, "O my son,
I miss the bright word in one
    Of thy measures and thy rhymes."
And Halfred the Scald replied,
"In another 'twas multiplied
    Three times."

Then King Olaf raised the hilt
Of iron, cross-shaped and gilt,
    And said, "Do not refuse;
Count well the gain and the loss,

Thor's hammer or Christ's cross:
    Choose!"

And Halfred the Scald said, "This
In the name of the Lord I kiss,
    Who on it was crucified!"
And a shout went round the board,
"In the name of Christ the Lord,
    Who died!"

Then over the waste of snows
The noonday sun uprose,
    Through the driving mists revealed,
Like the lifting of the Host,
By incense-clouds almost
    Concealed.

On the shining wall a vast
And shadowy cross was cast
    From the hilt of the lifted sword,
And in foaming cups of ale
The Berserks drank "Was-hael!
    To the Lord!"

The Building of the Long Serpent

Thorberg Skafting, master-builder,
    In his ship-yard by the sea,
Whistling, said, "It would bewilder
Any man but Thorberg Skafting,
    Any man but me!"

Near him lay the Dragon stranded,
    Built of old by Raud the Strong,
And King Olaf had commanded
He should build another Dragon,
    Twice as large and long.

Therefore whistled Thorberg Skafting,
    As he sat with half-closed eyes,
And his head turned sideways, drafting
That new vessel for King Olaf
    Twice the Dragon's size.

Round him busily hewed and hammered
    Mallet huge and heavy axe;
Workmen laughed and sang and clamored;
Whirred the wheels, that into rigging
    Spun the shining flax!

All this tumult heard the master,—
    It was music to his ear;
Fancy whispered all the faster,
"Men shall hear of Thorberg Skafting
    For a hundred year!"

Workmen sweating at the forges
    Fashioned iron bolt and bar,
Like a warlock's midnight orgies
Smoked and bubbled the black caldron
    With the boiling tar.

Did the warlocks mingle in it,
      Thorberg Skafting, any curse?
Could you not be gone a minute
But some mischief must be doing,
      Turning bad to worse?

'Twas an ill wind that came wafting,
      From his homestead words of woe
To his farm went Thorberg Skafting,
Oft repeating to his workmen,
      Build ye thus and so.

After long delays returning
      Came the master back by night
To his ship-yard longing, yearning,
Hurried he, and did not leave it
      Till the morning's light.

"Come and see my ship, my darling
      On the morrow" said the King;
"Finished now from keel to carling;
Never yet was seen in Norway
      Such a wondrous thing!"

In the ship-yard, idly talking,
      At the ship the workmen stared:
Some one, all their labor balking,
Down her sides had cut deep gashes,
      Not a plank was spared!

"Death be to the evil-doer!"
    With an oath King Olaf spoke;
"But rewards to his pursuer
And with wrath his face grew redder
    Than his scarlet cloak."

Straight the master-builder, smiling,
    Answered thus the angry King:
"Cease blaspheming and reviling,
Olaf, it was Thorberg Skafting
    Who has done this thing!"

Then he chipped and smoothed the planking,
    Till the King, delighted, swore,
With much lauding and much thanking,
"Handsomer is now my Dragon
    Than she was before!"

Seventy ells and four extended
    On the grass the vessel's keel;
High above it, gilt and splendid,
Rose the figure-head ferocious
    With its crest of steel.

Then they launched her from the tressels,
    In the ship-yard by the sea;
She was the grandest of all vessels,
Never ship was built in Norway
    Half so fine as she!

The Long Serpent was she christened,
    'Mid the roar of cheer on cheer!

They who to the Saga listened
Heard the name of Thorberg Skafting
    For a hundred year!

The Crew of the Long Serpent

Safe at anchor in Drontheim bay
King Olaf's fleet assembled lay,
    And, striped with white and blue,
Downward fluttered sail and banner,
As alights the screaming lanner;
Lustily cheered, in their wild manner,
    The Long Serpent's crew

Her forecastle man was Ulf the Red,
Like a wolf's was his shaggy head,
    His teeth as large and white;
His beard, of gray and russet blended,
Round as a swallow's nest descended;
As standard-bearer he defended
    Olaf's flag in the fight.

Near him Kolbiorn had his place,
Like the King in garb and face,
    So gallant and so hale;
Every cabin-boy and varlet
Wondered at his cloak of scarlet;
Like a river, frozen and star-lit,
    Gleamed his coat of mail.

By the bulkhead, tall and dark,
Stood Thrand Rame of Thelemark,
    A figure gaunt and grand;

On his hairy arm imprinted
Was an anchor, azure-tinted;
Like Thor's hammer, huge and dinted
   Was his brawny hand.

Einar Tamberskelver, bare
To the winds his golden hair,
   By the mainmast stood;
Graceful was his form, and slender,
And his eyes were deep and tender
As a woman's, in the splendor
   Of her maidenhood.

In the fore-hold Biorn and Bork
Watched the sailors at their work:
   Heavens! how they swore!
Thirty men they each commanded,
Iron-sinewed, horny-handed,
Shoulders broad, and chests expanded.
   Tugging at the oar.

These, and many more like these,
With King Olaf sailed the seas,
   Till the waters vast
Filled them with a vague devotion,
With the freedom and the motion,
With the roll and roar of ocean
   And the sounding blast.

When they landed from the fleet,
How they roared through Drontheim's street,
   Boisterous as the gale!

How they laughed and stamped and pounded,
Till the tavern roof resounded,
And the host looked on astounded
    As they drank the ale!

Never saw the wild North Sea
Such a gallant company
    Sail its billows blue!
Never, while they cruised and quarrelled,
Old King Gorm, or Blue-Tooth Harald,
Owned a ship so well apparelled,
    Boasted such a crew!

A Little Bird in the Air

A little bird in the air
    Is singing of Thyri the fair,
The sister of Svend the Dane;
And the song of the garrulous bird
In the streets of the town is heard,
    And repeated again and again.
        Hoist up your sails of silk,
        And flee away from each other.

To King Burislaf, it is said,
Was the beautiful Thyri wed,
    And a sorrowful bride went she;
And after a week and a day,
She has fled away and away,
    From his town by the stormy sea.
        Hoist up your sails of silk,
        And flee away from each other.

They say, that through heat and through cold,
Through weald, they say, and through wold,
   By day and by night, they say,
She has fled; and the gossips report
She has come to King Olaf's court,
   And the town is all in dismay.
      Hoist up your sails of silk,
      And flee away from each other.

It is whispered King Olaf has seen,
Has talked with the beautiful Queen;
   And they wonder how it will end;
For surely, if here she remain,
It is war with King Svend the Dane,
   And King Burislaf the Vend!
      Hoist up your sails of silk,
      And flee away from each other.

O, greatest wonder of all!
It is published in hamlet and hall,
   It roars like a flame that is fanned!
The King—yes, Olaf the King—
Has wedded her with his ring,
   And Thyri is Queen in the land!
      Hoist up your sails of silk,
      And flee away from each other.

Queen Thyri and the Angelica Stalks

Northward over Drontheim,
Flew the clamorous sea-gulls,
Sang the lark and linnet
   From the meadows green;

Weeping in her chamber,
Lonely and unhappy,
Sat the Drottning Thyri,
    Sat King Olaf's Queen.

In at all the windows
Streamed the pleasant sunshine,
On the roof above her
    Softly cooed the dove;

But the sound she heard not,
Nor the sunshine heeded,
For the thoughts of Thyri
    Were not thoughts of love,

Then King Olaf entered,
Beautiful as morning,
Like the sun at Easter
    Shone his happy face;

In his hand he carried
Angelicas uprooted,
With delicious fragrance
    Filling all the place.

Like a rainy midnight
Sat the Drottning Thyri,
Even the smile of Olaf
    Could not cheer her gloom;

Nor the stalks he gave her
With a gracious gesture,

And with words as pleasant
  As their own perfume.

In her hands he placed them,
And her jewelled fingers
Through the green leaves glistened
  Like the dews of morn;

But she cast them from her,
Haughty and indignant,
On the floor she threw them
  With a look of scorn.

"Richer presents," said she,
"Gave King Harald Gormson
To the Queen, my mother,
  Than such worthless weeds;"

"When he ravaged Norway,
Laying waste the kingdom,
Seizing scatt and treasure
  For her royal needs."

"But thou darest not venture
Through the Sound to Vendland,
My domains to rescue
  From King Burislaf;"

"Lest King Svend of Denmark,
Forked Beard, my brother,
Scatter all thy vessels
  As the wind the chaff."

Then up sprang King Olaf,
Like a reindeer bounding,
With an oath he answered
    Thus the luckless Queen:

"Never yet did Olaf
Fear King Svend of Denmark;
This right hand shall hale him
    By his forked chin!"

Then he left the chamber,
Thundering through the doorway,
Loud his steps resounded
    Down the outer stair.

Smarting with the insult,
Through the streets of Drontheim
Strode he red and wrathful,
    With his stately air.

All his ships he gathered,
Summoned all his forces,
Making his war levy
    In the region round;

Down the coast of Norway,
Like a flock of sea-gulls,
Sailed the fleet of Olaf
    Through the Danish Sound.

With his own hand fearless,
Steered he the Long Serpent,

Strained the creaking cordage,
   Bent each boom and gaff;

Till in Venland landing,
The domains of Thyri
He redeemed and rescued
   From King Burislaf.

Then said Olaf, laughing,
"Not ten yoke of oxen
Have the power to draw us
   Like a woman's hair!"

"Now will I confess it,
Better things are jewels
Than angelica stalks are
   For a Queen to wear."

King Svend of the Forked Beard

Loudly the sailors cheered
Svend of the Forked Beard,
As with his fleet he steered
   Southward to Vendland;
Where with their courses hauled
All were together called,
Under the Isle of Svald
   Near to the mainland.

After Queen Gunhild's death,
So the old Saga saith,
Plighted King Svend his faith
   To Sigrid the Haughty;

And to avenge his bride,
Soothing her wounded pride,
Over the waters wide
   King Olaf sought he.

Still on her scornful face,
Blushing with deep disgrace,
Bore she the crimson trace
   Of Olaf's gauntlet;
Like a malignant star,
Blazing in heaven afar,
Red shone the angry scar
   Under her frontlet.

Oft to King Svend she spake,
"For thine own honor's sake
Shalt thou swift vengeance take
   On the vile coward!"
Until the King at last,
Gusty and overcast,
Like a tempestuous blast
   Threatened and lowered.

Soon as the Spring appeared,
Svend of the Forked Beard
High his red standard reared,
   Eager for battle;
While every warlike Dane,
Seizing his arms again,
Left all unsown the grain,
   Unhoused the cattle.

Likewise the Swedish King
Summoned in haste a Thing,
Weapons and men to bring
    In aid of Denmark;
Eric the Norseman, too,
As the war-tidings flew,
Sailed with a chosen crew
    From Lapland and Finmark.

So upon Easter day
Sailed the three kings away,
Out of the sheltered bay,
    In the bright season;
With them Earl Sigvald came,
Eager for spoil and fame;
Pity that such a name
    Stooped to such treason!

Safe under Svald at last,
Now were their anchors cast,
Safe from the sea and blast,
    Plotted the three kings;
While, with a base intent,
Southward Earl Sigvald went,
On a foul errand bent,
    Unto the Sea-kings.

Thence to hold on his course,
Unto King Olaf's force,
Lying within the hoarse
    Mouths of Stet-haven;
Him to ensnare and bring,

Unto the Danish king,
Who his dead corse would fling
   Forth to the raven!

King Olaf and Earl Sigvald

On the gray sea-sands
King Olaf stands,
Northward and seaward
He points with his hands.

With eddy and whirl
The sea-tides curl,
Washing the sandals
Of Sigvald the Earl.

The mariners shout,
The ships swing about,
The yards are all hoisted,
The sails flutter out.

The war-horns are played,
The anchors are weighed,
Like moths in the distance
The sails flit and fade.

The sea is like lead
The harbor lies dead,
As a corse on the sea-shore,
Whose spirit has fled!

On that fatal day,
The histories say,

Seventy vessels
Sailed out of the bay.

But soon scattered wide
O'er the billows they ride,
While Sigvald and Olaf
Sail side by side.

Cried the Earl: "Follow me!
I your pilot will be,
For I know all the channels
Where flows the deep sea!"

So into the strait
Where his foes lie in wait,
Gallant King Olaf
Sails to his fate!
Then the sea-fog veils
The ships and their sails;
Queen Sigrid the Haughty,
Thy vengeance prevails!

King Olaf's War-Horns

"Strike the sails!" King Olaf said;
"Never shall men of mine take flight;
Never away from battle I fled,
Never away from my foes!
    Let God dispose
Of my life in the fight!"

"Sound the horns!" said Olaf the King;
And suddenly through the drifting brume

The blare of the horns began to ring,
Like the terrible trumpet shock
    Of Regnarock,
On the Day of Doom!

Louder and louder the war-horns sang
Over the level floor of the flood;
All the sails came down with a clang,
And there in the mist overhead
    The sun hung red
As a drop of blood.

Drifting down on the Danish fleet
Three together the ships were lashed,
So that neither should turn and retreat;
In the midst, but in front of the rest
    The burnished crest
Of the Serpent flashed.

King Olaf stood on the quarter-deck,
With bow of ash and arrows of oak,
His gilded shield was without a fleck,
His helmet inlaid with gold,
    And in many a fold
Hung his crimson cloak.

On the forecastle Ulf the Red
Watched the lashing of the ships;
"If the Serpent lie so far ahead,
We shall have hard work of it here,"
    Said he with a sneer
On his bearded lips.

King Olaf laid an arrow on string,
"Have I a coward on board?" said he.
"Shoot it another way, O King!"
Sullenly answered Ulf,
        The old sea-wolf;
"You have need of me!"

In front came Svend, the King of the Danes,
Sweeping down with his fifty rowers;
To the right, the Swedish king with his thanes;
And on board of the Iron Beard
        Earl Eric steered
To the left with his oars.

"These soft Danes and Swedes," said the King,
"At home with their wives had better stay,
Than come within reach of my Serpent's sting:
But where Eric the Norseman leads
        Heroic deeds
Will be done to-day!"

Then as together the vessels crashed,
Eric severed the cables of hide,
With which King Olaf's ships were lashed,
And left them to drive and drift
        With the currents swift
Of the outward tide.

Louder the war-horns growl and snarl,
Sharper the dragons bite and sting!
Eric the son of Hakon Jarl
A death-drink salt as the sea

Pledges to thee,
Olaf the King!

Einar Tamberskelver

It was Einar Tamberskelver
   Stood beside the mast;
From his yew-bow, tipped with silver,
   Flew the arrows fast;
Aimed at Eric unavailing,
   As he sat concealed,
Half behind the quarter-railing,
   Half behind his shield.

First an arrow struck the tiller,
   Just above his head;
"Sing, O Eyvind Skaldaspiller,"
   Then Earl Eric said.
"Sing the song of Hakon dying,
   Sing his funeral wail!"
And another arrow flying
   Grazed his coat of mail.

Turning to a Lapland yeoman,
   As the arrow passed,
Said Earl Eric, "Shoot that bowman
   Standing by the mast."
Sooner than the word was spoken
   Flew the yeoman's shaft;
Einar's bow in twain was broken,
   Einar only laughed.

"What was that?" said Olaf, standing
    On the quarter-deck.
"Something heard I like the stranding
    Of a shattered wreck."
Einar then, the arrow taking
    From the loosened string,
Answered, "That was Norway breaking
    From thy hand, O King!"

"Thou art but a poor diviner,"
    Straightway Olaf said;
"Take my bow, and swifter, Einar,
    Let thy shafts be sped."
Of his bows the fairest choosing,
    Reached he from above;
Einar saw the blood-drops oozing
    Through his iron glove.

But the bow was thin and narrow;
    At the first assay,
O'er its head he drew the arrow,
    Flung the bow away;
Said, with hot and angry temper
    Flushing in his cheek,
"Olaf! for so great a Kämper
    Are thy bows too weak!"

Then, with smile of joy defiant
    On his beardless lip,
Scaled he, light and self-reliant,
    Eric's dragon-ship.
Loose his golden locks were flowing,

Bright his armor gleamed;
Like Saint Michael overthrowing
    Lucifer he seemed.

King Olaf's Death-drink

All day has the battle raged,
All day have the ships engaged,
But not yet is assuaged
    The vengeance of Eric the Earl.

The decks with blood are red,
The arrows of death are sped,
The ships are filled with the dead,
    And the spears the champions hurl.

They drift as wrecks on the tide,
The grappling-irons are plied,
The boarders climb up the side,
    The shouts are feeble and few.

Ah! never shall Norway again
See her sailors come back o'er the main;
They all lie wounded or slain,
    Or asleep in the billows blue!

On the deck stands Olaf the King,
Around him whistle and sing
The spears that the foemen fling,
    And the stones they hurl with their hands.

In the midst of the stones and the spears,
Kolbiorn, the marshal, appears,

His shield in the air he uprears,
  By the side of King Olaf he stands.

Over the slippery wreck
Of the Long Serpent's deck
Sweeps Eric with hardly a check,
  His lips with anger are pale;

He hews with his axe at the mast,
Till it falls, with the sails overcast,
Like a snow-covered pine in the vast
  Dim forests of Orkadale.

Seeking King Olaf then,
He rushes aft with his men,
As a hunter into the den
  Of the bear, when he stands at bay.

"Remember Jarl Hakon!" he cries;
When lo! on his wondering eyes,
Two kingly figures arise,
  Two Olafs in warlike array!

Then Kolbiorn speaks in the ear
Of King Olaf a word of cheer,
In a whisper that none may hear,
  With a smile on his tremulous lip;

Two shields raised high in the air,
Two flashes of golden hair,
Two scarlet meteors' glare,
  And both have leaped from the ship.

Earl Eric's men in the boats
Seize Kolbiorn's shield as it floats,
And cry, from their hairy throats,
   "See! it is Olaf the King!"

While far on the opposite side
Floats another shield on the tide,
Like a jewel set in the wide
   Sea-current's eddying ring.

There is told a wonderful tale,
How the King stripped off his mail,
Like leaves of the brown sea-kale,
   As he swam beneath the main;

But the young grew old and gray,
And never, by night or by day,
In his kingdom of Norroway
   Was King Olaf seen again!

The Nun of Nidaros

In the convent of Drontheim,
Alone in her chamber
Knelt Astrid the Abbess,
At midnight, adoring,
Beseeching, entreating
The Virgin and Mother.

She heard in the silence
The voice of one speaking,
Without in the darkness,
In gusts of the night-wind

Now louder, now nearer,
Now lost in the distance.

The voice of a stranger
It seemed as she listened,
Of some one who answered,
Beseeching, imploring,
A cry from afar off
She could not distinguish.

The voice of Saint John,
The beloved disciple,
Who wandered and waited
The Master's appearance.
Alone in the darkness,
Unsheltered and friendless.

"It is accepted,
The angry defiance,
The challenge of battle!
It is accepted,
But not with the weapons
Of war that thou wieldest!"

"Cross against corselet,
Love against hatred,
Peace-cry for war-cry!
Patience is powerful;
He that o'ercometh
Hath power o'er the nations!"

"As torrents in summer,
Half dried in their channels,
Suddenly rise, though the
Sky is still cloudless,
For rain has been falling
Far off at their fountains;"

"So hearts that are fainting
Grow full to o'erflowing,
And they that behold it
Marvel, and know not
That God at their fountains
Far off has been raining!"

"Stronger than steel
Is the sword of the Spirit;
Swifter than arrows
The light of the truth is,
Greater than anger
Is love, and subdueth!"

"Thou art a phantom,
A shape of the sea-mist,
A shape of the brumal
Rain, and the darkness
Fearful and formless;
Day dawns and thou art not!"

"The dawn is not distant,
Nor is the night starless;
Love is eternal!
God is still God, and

His faith shall not fail us
Christ is eternal!"

Snow-Flakes

Out of the bosom of the Air,
    Out of the cloud-folds of her garments shaken,
Over the woodlands brown and bare,
    Over the harvest-fields forsaken,
      Silent, and soft, and slow
      Descends the snow.

Even as our cloudy fancies take
    Suddenly shape in some divine expression,
Even as the troubled heart doth make
    In the white countenance confession,
      The troubled sky reveals
      The grief it feels.

This is the poem of the air,
    Slowly in silent syllables recorded;
This is the secret of despair,
    Long in its cloudy bosom hoarded,
      Now whispered and revealed
      To wood and field.

Paul Revere's Ride

Listen, my children, and you shall hear
Of the midnight ride of Paul Revere,
On the eighteenth of April, in Seventy-five;
Hardly a man is now alive
Who remembers that famous day and year.

He said to his friend, "If the British march
By land or sea from the town to-night,
Hang a lantern aloft in the belfry arch
Of the North Church tower as a signal light,—
One, if by land, and two, if by sea;
And I on the opposite shore will be,
Ready to ride and spread the alarm
Through every Middlesex village and farm,
For the country folk to be up and to arm."

Then he said, "Good night!" and with muffled oar
Silently rowed to the Charlestown shore,
Just as the moon rose over the bay,
Where swinging wide at her moorings lay
The Somerset, British man-of-war;
A phantom ship, with each mast and spar
Across the moon like a prison bar,
And a huge black hulk, that was magnified
By its own reflection in the tide.

Meanwhile, his friend, through alley and street,
Wanders and watches with eager ears,
Till in the silence around him he hears
The muster of men at the barrack door,

The sound of arms, and the tramp of feet,
And the measured tread of the grenadiers,
Marching down to their boats on the shore.

Then he climbed the tower of the Old North Church,
By the wooden stairs, with stealthy tread,
To the belfry-chamber overhead,
And startled the pigeons from their perch
On the sombre rafters, that round him made
Masses and moving shapes of shade,—
By the trembling ladder, steep and tall,
To the highest window in the wall,
Where he paused to listen and look down
A moment on the roofs of the town,
And the moonlight flowing over all.

Beneath, in the churchyard, lay the dead,
In their night-encampment on the hill,
Wrapped in silence so deep and still
That he could hear, like a sentinel's tread,
The watchful night-wind, as it went
Creeping along from tent to tent,
And seeming to whisper, "All is well!"
A moment only he feels the spell
Of the place and the hour, and the secret dread
Of the lonely belfry and the dead;
For suddenly all his thoughts are bent
On a shadowy something far away,
Where the river widens to meet the bay,—
A line of black that bends and floats
On the rising tide, like a bridge of boats.
Meanwhile, impatient to mount and ride,

Booted and spurred, with a heavy stride
On the opposite shore walked Paul Revere.
Now he patted his horse's side,
Now gazed at the landscape far and near,
Then, impetuous, stamped the earth,
And turned and tightened his saddle girth;
But mostly he watched with eager search
The belfry-tower of the Old North Church,
As it rose above the graves on the hill,
Lonely and spectral and sombre and still.
And lo! as he looks, on the belfry's height
A glimmer, and then a gleam of light!
He springs to the saddle, the bridle he turns,
But lingers and gazes, till full on his sight
A second lamp in the belfry burns!

A hurry of hoofs in a village street,
A shape in the moonlight, a bulk in the dark,
And beneath, from the pebbles, in passing, a spark
Struck out by a steed flying fearless and fleet:
That was all! And yet, through the gloom and the light,
The fate of a nation was riding that night;
And the spark struck out by that steed, in his flight,
Kindled the land into flame with its heat.

He has left the village and mounted the steep,
And beneath him, tranquil and broad and deep,
Is the Mystic, meeting the ocean tides;
And under the alders, that skirt its edge,
Now soft on the sand, now loud on the ledge,
Is heard the tramp of his steed as he rides.
It was twelve by the village clock,

When he crossed the bridge into Medford town.
He heard the crowing of the cock,
And the barking of the farmer's dog,
And felt the damp of the river fog,
That rises after the sun goes down.

It was one by the village clock,
When he galloped into Lexington.
He saw the gilded weathercock
Swim in the moonlight as he passed,
And the meeting-house windows, blank and bare,
Gaze at him with a spectral glare,
As if they already stood aghast
At the bloody work they would look upon.

It was two by the village clock,
When he came to the bridge in Concord town.
He heard the bleating of the flock,
And the twitter of birds among the trees,
And felt the breath of the morning breeze
Blowing over the meadows brown.
And one was safe and asleep in his bed
Who at the bridge would be first to fall,
Who that day would be lying dead,
Pierced by a British musket-ball.

You know the rest. In the books you have read,
How the British Regulars fired and fled,—
How the farmers gave them ball for ball,
From behind each fence and farm-yard wall,
Chasing the red-coats down the lane,
Then crossing the fields to emerge again

Under the trees at the turn of the road,
And only pausing to fire and load.

So through the night rode Paul Revere;
And so through the night went his cry of alarm
To every Middlesex village and farm,—
A cry of defiance and not of fear,
A voice in the darkness, a knock at the door,
And a word that shall echo forevermore!
For, borne on the night-wind of the Past,
Through all our history, to the last,
In the hour of darkness and peril and need,
The people will waken and listen to hear
The hurrying hoof-beats of that steed,
And the midnight message of Paul Revere.

Aftermath

When the summer fields are mown,
When the birds are fledged and flown,
    And the dry leaves strew the path;
With the falling of the snow,
With the cawing of the crow,
Once again the fields we mow
    And gather in the aftermath.

Not the sweet, new grass with flowers
Is this harvesting of ours;
    Not the upland clover bloom;
But the rowen mixed with weeds,
Tangled tufts from marsh and meads,
Where the poppy drops its seeds
    In the silence and the gloom.

Morituri Salutamus

"O Caesar, we who are about to die
Salute you!" was the gladiators' cry
In the arena, standing face to face
With death and with the Roman populace.

O ye familiar scenes,—ye groves of pine,
That once were mine and are no longer mine,—
Thou river, widening through the meadows green
To the vast sea, so near and yet unseen,—
Ye halls, in whose seclusion and repose
Phantoms of fame, like exhalations, rose
And vanished,—we who are about to die,
Salute you; earth and air and sea and sky,
And the Imperial Sun that scatters down
His sovereign splendors upon grove and town.

Ye do not answer us! ye do not hear!
We are forgotten; and in your austere
And calm indifference, ye little care
Whether we come or go, or whence or where.
What passing generations fill these halls,
What passing voices echo from these walls,
Ye heed not; we are only as the blast,
A moment heard, and then forever past.

Not so the teachers who in earlier days
Led our bewildered feet through learning's maze;
They answer us—alas! what have I said?
What greetings come there from the voiceless dead?
What salutation, welcome, or reply?

What pressure from the hands that lifeless lie?
They are no longer here; they all are gone
Into the land of shadows,—all save one.
Honor and reverence, and the good repute
That follows faithful service as its fruit,
Be unto him, whom living we salute.

The great Italian poet, when he made
His dreadful journey to the realms of shade,
Met there the old instructor of his youth,
And cried in tones of pity and of ruth:
"Oh, never from the memory of my heart
Your dear, paternal image shall depart,
Who while on earth, ere yet by death surprised,
Taught me how mortals are immortalized;
How grateful am I for that patient care
All my life long my language shall declare."

To-day we make the poet's words our own
And utter them in plaintive undertone;
Nor to the living only be they said,
But to the other living called the dead,
Whose dear, paternal images appear
Not wrapped in gloom, but robed in sunshine here;
Whose simple lives, complete and without flaw,
Were part and parcel of great Nature's law;
Who said not to their Lord, as if afraid
"Here is thy talent in a napkin laid,"
But labored in their sphere, as men who live
In the delight that work alone can give.
Peace be to them; eternal peace and rest,
And the fulfilment of the great behest:

"Ye have been faithful over a few things,
Over ten cities shall ye reign as kings."

And ye who fill the places we once filled,
And follow in the furrows that we tilled,
Young men, whose generous hearts are beating high,
We who are old, and are about to die,
Salute you; hail you; take your hands in ours,
And crown you with our welcome as with flowers!

How beautiful is youth! how bright it gleams
With its illusions, aspirations, dreams!
Book of Beginnings, Story without End,
Each maid a heroine, and each man a friend!
Aladdin's Lamp, and Fortunatus' Purse,
That holds the treasures of the universe!
All possibilities are in its hands,
No danger daunts it, and no foe withstands;
In its sublime audacity of faith,
"Be thou removed!" it to the mountain saith,
And with ambitious feet, secure and proud,
Ascends the ladder leaning on the cloud!

As ancient Priam at the Scaean gate
Sat on the walls of Troy in regal state
With the old men, too old and weak to fight,
Chirping like grasshoppers in their delight
To see the embattled hosts, with spear and shield,
Of Trojans and Achaians in the field;
So from the snowy summits of our years
We see you in the plain, as each appears,
And question of you; asking, "Who is he

That towers above the others? Which may be
Atreides, Menelaus, Odysseus,
Ajax the great, or bold Idomeneus?"

Let him not boast who puts his armor on
As he who puts it off, the battle done.
Study yourselves; and most of all note well
Wherein kind Nature meant you to excel.
Not every blossom ripens into fruit;
Minerva, the inventress of the flute,
Flung it aside, when she her face surveyed
Distorted in a fountain as she played;
The unlucky Marsyas found it, and his fate
Was one to make the bravest hesitate.

Write on your doors the saying wise and old,
"Be bold! be bold!" and everywhere,—"Be bold;
Be not too bold!" Yet better the excess
Than the defect; better the more than less;
Better like Hector in the field to die,
Than like a perfumed Paris turn and fly.

And now, my classmates; ye remaining few
That number not the half of those we knew,
Ye, against whose familiar names not yet
The fatal asterisk of death is set,
Ye I salute! The horologe of Time
Strikes the half-century with a solemn chime,
And summons us together once again,
The joy of meeting not unmixed with pain.

Where are the others? Voices from the deep
Caverns of darkness answer me: "They sleep!"
I name no names; instinctively I feel
Each at some well-remembered grave will kneel,
And from the inscription wipe the weeds and moss,
For every heart best knoweth its own loss.
I see their scattered gravestones gleaming white
Through the pale dusk of the impending night;
O'er all alike the impartial sunset throws
Its golden lilies mingled with the rose;
We give to each a tender thought, and pass
Out of the graveyards with their tangled grass,
Unto these scenes frequented by our feet
When we were young, and life was fresh and sweet.

What shall I say to you? What can I say
Better than silence is? When I survey
This throng of faces turned to meet my own,
Friendly and fair, and yet to me unknown,
Transformed the very landscape seems to be;
It is the same, yet not the same to me.
So many memories crowd upon my brain,
So many ghosts are in the wooded plain,
I fain would steal away, with noiseless tread,
As from a house where some one lieth dead.
I cannot go;—I pause;—I hesitate;
My feet reluctant linger at the gate;
As one who struggles in a troubled dream
To speak and cannot, to myself I seem.

Vanish the dream! Vanish the idle fears!
Vanish the rolling mists of fifty years!

Whatever time or space may intervene,
I will not be a stranger in this scene.
Here every doubt, all indecision, ends;
Hail, my companions, comrades, classmates, friends!

Ah me! the fifty years since last we met
Seem to me fifty folios bound and set
By Time, the great transcriber, on his shelves,
Wherein are written the histories of ourselves.
What tragedies, what comedies, are there;
What joy and grief, what rapture and despair!
What chronicles of triumph and defeat,
Of struggle, and temptation, and retreat!
What records of regrets, and doubts, and fears
What pages blotted, blistered by our tears!
What lovely landscapes on the margin shine,
What sweet, angelic faces, what divine
And holy images of love and trust,
Undimmed by age, unsoiled by damp or dust!

Whose hand shall dare to open and explore
These volumes, closed and clasped forevermore?
Not mine. With reverential feet I pass;
I hear a voice that cries, "Alas! alas!
Whatever hath been written shall remain,
Nor be erased nor written o'er again;
The unwritten only still belongs to thee:
Take heed, and ponder well what that shall be."

As children frightened by a thunder-cloud
Are reassured if some one reads aloud
A tale of wonder, with enchantment fraught,

Or wild adventure, that diverts their thought,
Let me endeavor with a tale to chase
The gathering shadows of the time and place,
And banish what we all too deeply feel
Wholly to say, or wholly to conceal.

In mediaeval Rome, I know not where,
There stood an image with its arm in air,
And on its lifted finger, shining clear,
A golden ring with the device, "Strike here!"
Greatly the people wondered, though none guessed
The meaning that these words but half expressed,
Until a learned clerk, who at noonday
With downcast eyes was passing on his way,
Paused, and observed the spot, and marked it well,
Whereon the shadow of the finger fell;
And, coming back at midnight, delved, and found
A secret stairway leading underground.
Down this he passed into a spacious hall,
Lit by a flaming jewel on the wall;
And opposite, in threatening attitude,
With bow and shaft a brazen statue stood.
Upon its forehead, like a coronet,
Were these mysterious words of menace set:
"That which I am, I am; my fatal aim
None can escape, not even yon luminous flame!"

Midway the hall was a fair table placed,
With cloth of gold, and golden cups enchased
With rubies, and the plates and knives were gold,
And gold the bread and viands manifold.
Around it, silent, motionless, and sad,

Were seated gallant knights in armor clad,
And ladies beautiful with plume and zone,
But they were stone, their hearts within were stone;
And the vast hall was filled in every part
With silent crowds, stony in face and heart.

Long at the scene, bewildered and amazed
The trembling clerk in speechless wonder gazed;
Then from the table, by his greed made bold,
He seized a goblet and a knife of gold,
And suddenly from their seats the guests upsprang,
The vaulted ceiling with loud clamors rang,
The archer sped his arrow, at their call,
Shattering the lambent jewel on the wall,
And all was dark around and overhead;—
Stark on the door the luckless clerk lay dead!

The writer of this legend then records
Its ghostly application in these words:
The image is the Adversary old,
Whose beckoning finger points to realms of gold;
Our lusts and passions are the downward stair
That leads the soul from a diviner air;
The archer, Death; the flaming jewel, Life;
Terrestrial goods, the goblet and the knife;
The knights and ladies, all whose flesh and bone
By avarice have been hardened into stone;
The clerk, the scholar whom the love of pelf
Tempts from his books and from his nobler self.

The scholar and the world! The endless strife,
The discord in the harmonies of life!

The love of learning, the sequestered nooks,
And all the sweet serenity of books;
The market-place, the eager love of gain,
Whose aim is vanity, and whose end is pain!

But why, you ask me, should this tale be told
To men grown old, or who are growing old?
It is too late! Ah, nothing is too late
Till the tired heart shall cease to palpitate.
Cato learned Greek at eighty; Sophocles
Wrote his grand Oedipus, and Simonides
Bore off the prize of verse from his compeers,
When each had numbered more than fourscore years,
And Theophrastus, at fourscore and ten,
Had but begun his "Characters of Men."
Chaucer, at Woodstock with the nightingales,
At sixty wrote the Canterbury Tales;
Goethe at Weimar, toiling to the last,
Completed Faust when eighty years were past.
These are indeed exceptions; but they show
How far the gulf-stream of our youth may flow
Into the arctic regions of our lives.
Where little else than life itself survives.

As the barometer foretells the storm
While still the skies are clear, the weather warm,
So something in us, as old age draws near,
Betrays the pressure of the atmosphere.
The nimble mercury, ere we are aware,
Descends the elastic ladder of the air;
The telltale blood in artery and vein
Sinks from its higher levels in the brain;

Whatever poet, orator, or sage
May say of it, old age is still old age.
It is the waning, not the crescent moon;
The dusk of evening, not the blaze of noon;
It is not strength, but weakness; not desire,
But its surcease; not the fierce heat of fire,
The burning and consuming element,
But that of ashes and of embers spent,
In which some living sparks we still discern,
Enough to warm, but not enough to burn.

What then? Shall we sit idly down and say
The night hath come; it is no longer day?
The night hath not yet come; we are not quite
Cut off from labor by the failing light;
Something remains for us to do or dare;
Even the oldest tree some fruit may bear;
Not Oedipus Coloneus, or Greek Ode,
Or tales of pilgrims that one morning rode
Out of the gateway of the Tabard Inn,
But other something, would we but begin;
For age is opportunity no less
Than youth itself, though in another dress,
And as the evening twilight fades away
The sky is filled with stars, invisible by day.

The Sermon of St Francis

Up soared the lark into the air,
A shaft of song, a winged prayer,
As if a soul, released from pain,
Were flying back to heaven again.

St. Francis heard; it was to him
An emblem of the Seraphim;
The upward motion of the fire,
The light, the heat, the heart's desire.

Around Assisi's convent gate
The birds, God's poor who cannot wait,
From moor and mere and darksome wood
Came flocking for their dole of food.

"O brother birds," St. Francis said,
"Ye come to me and ask for bread,
But not with bread alone to-day
Shall ye be fed and sent away.

"Ye shall be fed, ye happy birds,
With manna of celestial words;
Not mine, though mine they seem to be,
Not mine, though they be spoken through me.

"O, doubly are ye bound to praise
The great Creator in your lays;
He giveth you your plumes of down,
Your crimson hoods, your cloaks of brown.

"He giveth you your wings to fly
And breathe a purer air on high,
And careth for you everywhere,
Who for yourselves so little care!"

With flutter of swift wings and songs
Together rose the feathered throngs,
And singing scattered far apart;
Deep peace was in St. Francis' heart.

He knew not if the brotherhood
His homily had understood;
He only knew that to one ear
The meaning of his words was clear.

Nature

As a fond mother, when the day is o'er,
    Leads by the hand her little child to bed,
    Half willing, half reluctant to be led,
    And leave his broken playthings on the floor,
Still gazing at them through the open door,
    Nor wholly reassured and comforted
    By promises of others in their stead,
    Which, though more splendid, may not please him
        more;
So Nature deals with us, and takes away
    Our playthings one by one, and by the hand
    Leads us to rest so gently, that we go
Scarce knowing if we wish to go or stay,
    Being too full of sleep to understand
    How far the unknown transcends the what we know.

Venice

White swan of cities, slumbering in thy nest
 So wonderfully built among the reeds
 Of the lagoon, that fences thee and feeds,
 As sayeth thy old historian and thy guest!
White water-lily, cradled and caressed
 By ocean streams, and from the silt and weeds
 Lifting thy golden filaments and seeds,
 Thy sun-illumined spires, thy crown and crest!
White phantom city, whose untrodden streets
 Are rivers, and whose pavements are the shifting
 Shadows of palaces and strips of sky;
I wait to see thee vanish like the fleets
 Seen in mirage, or towers of cloud uplifting
 In air their unsubstantial masonry.

Holidays

The holiest of all holidays are those
  Kept by ourselves in silence and apart;
  The secret anniversaries of the heart,
  When the full river of feeling overflows;—
The happy days unclouded to their close;
  The sudden joys that out of darkness start
  As flames from ashes; swift desires that dart
  Like swallows singing down each wind that blows!
White as the gleam of a receding sail,
  White as a cloud that floats and fades in air,
  White as the whitest lily on a stream,
These tender memories are;—a Fairy Tale
  Of some enchanted land we know not where,
  But lovely as a landscape in a dream.

The Three Silences of Molinos

To John Greenleaf Whittier

Three Silences there are: the first of speech,
    The second of desire, the third of thought;
    This is the lore a Spanish monk, distraught
    With dreams and visions, was the first to teach.
These Silences, commingling each with each,
    Made up the perfect Silence, that he sought
    And prayed for, and wherein at times he caught
    Mysterious sounds from realms beyond our reach.
O thou, whose daily life anticipates
    The life to come, and in whose thought and word
    The spiritual world preponderates.
Hermit of Amesbury! thou too hast heard
    Voices and melodies from beyond the gates,
    And speakest only when thy soul is stirred!

The Cross of Snow

In the long, sleepless watches of the night,
    A gentle face—the face of one long dead—
    Looks at me from the wall, where round its head
    The night-lamp casts a halo of pale light.
Here in this room she died; and soul more white
    Never through martyrdom of fire was led
    To its repose; nor can in books be read
    The legend of a life more benedight.
There is a mountain in the distant West
    That, sun-defying, in its deep ravines
    Displays a cross of snow upon its side.
Such is the cross I wear upon my breast
    These eighteen years, through all the changing
        scenes
    And seasons, changeless since the day she died.

The Tide Rises, The Tide Falls

The tide rises, the tide falls,
The twilight darkens, the curlew calls;
Along the sea-sands damp and brown
The traveller hastens toward the town,
    And the tide rises, the tide falls.

Darkness settles on roofs and walls,
But the sea, the sea in the darkness calls;
The little waves, with their soft, white hands,
Efface the footprints in the sands,
    And the tide rises, the tide falls.

The morning breaks; the steeds in their stalls
Stamp and neigh, as the hostler calls;
The day returns, but nevermore
Returns the traveller to the shore,
    And the tide rises, the tide falls.

Becalmed

Becalmed upon the sea of Thought,
Still unattained the land it sought,
My mind, with loosely-hanging sails,
Lies waiting the auspicious gales.

On either side, behind, before,
The ocean stretches like a floor,—
A level floor of amethyst,
Crowned by a golden dome of mist.

Blow, breath of inspiration, blow!
Shake and uplift this golden glow!
And fill the canvas of the mind
With wafts of thy celestial wind.

Blow, breath of song! until I feel
The straining sail, the lifting keel,
The life of the awakening sea,
Its motion and its mystery!

Index of First Lines

In the heroic days when Ferdinand 143
In the long, sleepless watches of the night 230
In the market-place of Bruges stands the belfry old and brown 54
It was the schooner Hesperus 37

Listen, my children, and you shall hear 208
Lo! in the painted oriel of the West 71
Loud he sang the psalm of David! 41

"O Caesar, we who are about to die 214
Oft have I seen at some cathedral door 135
Often I think of the beautiful town 125
Oh the long and dreary Winter! 111
Out of the bosom of the Air 207

River! that in silence windest 49

Saint Augustine! well hast thou said 129
Spake full well, in language quaint and olden 20
"Speak! speak! thou fearful guest! 31

Tell me not, in mournful numbers 18
The day is cold, and dark, and dreary 48
The day is done, and the darkness 61
The day is ending 68
The holiest of all holidays are those 228
The night is come, but not too soon 27
The rising moon has hid the stars 46
The shades of night were falling fast 52
The tide rises, the tide falls 231

There is a Reaper, whose name is Death   29
This is the Arsenal. From floor to ceiling   66
This is the forest primeval. The murmuring pines and the
   hemlocks   75
This is the place. Stand still, my steed   72
Three Silences there are: the first of speech   229
Two angels, one of Life and one of Death,   139

Under a spreading chestnut-tree   44
Up soared the lark into the air   224

We sat within the farm-house old   79
When descends on the Atlantic   95
When the hours of Day are numbered   16
When the summer fields are mown   213
When winter winds are piercing chill   12
White swan of cities, slumbering in thy nest   227
With what a glory comes and goes the year!   10